THE CREATIVE COOK

Tempting

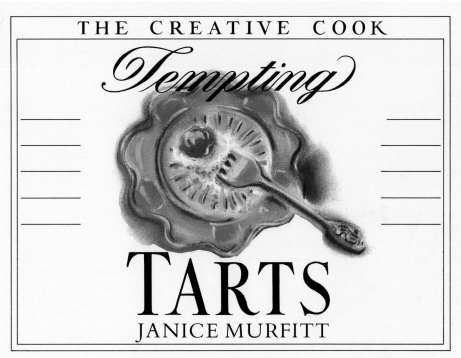

TARTS

JANICE MURFITT

FOREWORD BY ALBERT ROUX

PHOTOGRAPHY BY MICHELLE GARRETT

CONRAN OCTOPUS

*To Richard, Emma and Anna for all their help
and support and for tasting all the recipes.*

Please note the following:

Quantities given in all the recipes serve 4 people unless otherwise stated.

Spoon measurements are level unless otherwise stated.

Metric and imperial measures are both given, use one or the other as the two are not interchangeable.

Flour used is plain white flour, unless otherwise specified.

Preparation of ingredients, such as the cleaning, trimming and peeling of vegetables and fruit, is presumed and the text only refers to any aspect of this if unusual, such as onions used unpeeled etc.

Citrus fruit is generally coated in a layer of preservative wax. For this reason, whenever a recipe uses the rind of oranges, lemons or limes the text specifies unwaxed fruit. If organic uncoated fruit is not available, scrub the fruit vigorously in hot soapy water, rinse well and pat dry.

Eggs used are size 3 (65 g/2¼ oz) unless otherwise specified. The Government recommends that eggs not be consumed raw, and people most at risk, such as children, old people, invalids and pregnant women, should not eat them lightly cooked. This book includes recipes with raw and lightly cooked eggs, which should not be eaten by the above categories. These recipes are marked by a * in the text. Once prepared, these dishes should be kept refrigerated and used promptly.

Editorial Direction: Lewis Esson Publishing
Art Director: Mary Evans
Design: Sue Storey
Illustrations: Alison Barratt
Food for Photography: Janice Murfitt
Styling: Róisín Nield
Editorial Assistant: Penny David
Production: Julia Golding

First published in 1992 by
Conran Octopus Limited,
37 Shelton Street, London WC2H 9HN

This new edition published in 1993 by
Conran Octopus Limited.

British Library Cataloguing in
Publication Data
A catalogue record for this book is available from the
British Library

ISBN 1-85029-435-6

Typeset by Hunters Armley Ltd
Printed and bound in Hong Kong.

CONTENTS

FOREWORD

For someone like me, dedicated to good food, the concept of the tart conjures up nostalgic images of treacle, home-made strawberry jam, sliced apples, fresh nuts, egg and ham, prime mince meat and so on. Since my youth, a good tart with a thin crisp pastry base and rich flavoursome filling has always been high on my list of favourite foods. This may, of course, be one of the reasons that I chose to start my career as a chef by training as an apprentice *pâtissier,* or pastry chef.

These new books in the *Creative Cook* series are among the most exciting cookbooks I have seen in a long while. They reflect in a timely manner the full effects of the recent welcome change in the eating habits of the majority of people in this country – as well as being healthier they are more open to new ideas, receptive to fresh influences and ready to experiment with interesting new ingredients.

In *Tempting Tarts,* Janice Murfitt provides new and unusual ways of adding flavour and interest to the basic pastries used, like adding crushed nuts or citrus zest, and also presents a rather splendid array of fillings, both comfortingly traditional and classic with an intriguing twist. With these recipes she at long last gives tarts, sweet and savoury, the recognition they deserve. As well as perfect treats to accompany tea and coffee, they make wonderful desserts, exciting starters, satisfying and healthy light meals and memorable party food.

Happy cooking!

ALBERT ROUX

INTRODUCTION

Sweet tarts are irresistible . . . jewel-bright fruit tarts decked with luscious berries and glazed with jam; or luscious rich honeyed mixtures studded with nuts and thickly dusted with icing sugar to give a delicate appearance, yet hint at the delights hidden beneath . . . the temptation they present is overwhelming.

Savoury tarts, often referred to as flans or quiches, may also contain wonderful blends of herbs, vegetables, seafood, poultry or meat, all set in a rich creamy sauce to make the most satisfying of starters, light meals or party snacks.

It is the pastry which holds and contains all these various fillings and sets them off by providing wonderfully satisfying contrasts of textures. It may be formed and baked into many shapes and sizes and will offer dif-ferent textures and flavours depending on the recipe.

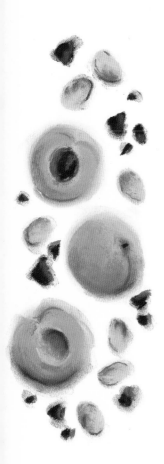

TYPES OF PASTRY

Plain shortcrust pastry, which is the pastry most commonly used for savoury tarts, is made with flour, white fat and water and produces a crisp tart base. If the fats are changed (to say all butter or a mixture of half margarine and half white fat), it is quite noticeable how the pastry texture and flavour changes.

The addition of eggs, fruit juices, yogurt or sour cream makes a richer pastry which, when baked, produces a crisp light and flaky result. When sugar is added to make a sweet shortcrust the tart cases become almost like shortbread in texture and during baking colour much more quickly.

Many flavouring ingredients may be introduced into the pastry, such as nuts, grated citrus zest, spices, chocolate, herbs and seasonings. This not only adds variety to the taste and texture of the pastry cases but, teamed with the appropriate fillings, such flavoured pastries can give an endless variety of wonderful flavour combinations.

MAKING PASTRY

Pastry is very simple to make, but unless care is taken when handling the dough, problems – such as uneven and shrunken pastry cases or hard dense textures – can arise. Most such pitfalls may be avoided by simply following a few easy guidelines when making the pastry:

★ Make sure all the ingredients are cold.
★ Weigh all the ingredients carefully beforehand.
★ Sift the flour into a bowl first to add more air to the mixture and thus give lighter results.
★ Use fat which is cold and cut into pieces, so that when it is rubbed into the flour it breaks down evenly into fine 'crumbs' and does not form a sticky heavy mixture.
★ Add the measured amount of cold or chilled liquid gradually, mixing well with a fork until the mixture begins to bind together. Too much liquid makes a hard pastry which shrinks during cooking.
★ On a lightly floured surface, knead the mixture lightly with the fingertips until the dough is smooth and free from cracks. Do not over-knead with hot hands. Use the dough immediately or wrap it in film and keep it in a cool place until it is required.

A food processor may be used to make the pastry but take care not to over-work the mixture or it will form into a dough before the correct quantity of liquid has been added, which will produce pastry that is too short and very hard to handle.

ROLLING AND LINING

Roll out the pastry evenly on a lightly floured surface, keeping it in a good neat shape which as far as possible more or less matches the shape of the tin to be lined, whatever its size. Always roll only to and from you, never at angles or from side to side. Roll two or three times, then give the pastry a 90 degree turn and repeat the process. Keep doing this until the pastry is the right size and shape, or 2.5 cm/1 in larger all round than the tin to be lined.

Never stretch the pastry or it will shrink back during cooking to produce an uneven pastry case.

To line a tart tin, support the sheet of pastry over a rolling pin and arrange it over the base of the tin, easing it into the corners. Then press it gently up the sides. Trim off the excess and press the sides of the pastry into any flutes on the sides of the tin.

When lining small tartlets and barquette tins, arrange them closely on a baking sheet and then place the sheet of pastry loosely over the top. Using a little ball of pastry, ease the pastry sheet into each tin and then run the rolling pin over the tops lightly to cut off the excess. Finish the edges with a fork or the fingers.

Always prick the base of pastry cases all over with a fork to ensure that the pastry remains flat during cooking. Chill for at least 30 minutes to 1 hour – or even overnight – before cooking to give the pastry time to rest. It will then retain its shape better during cooking. However, do remember that a cold pastry base will take longer to cook.

BAKING BLIND

It is usually a good idea to pre-bake a pastry case before filling it, especially if it is to have very liquid filling. Such 'baking blind' ensures that the base is cooked and crisp and prevents the filling from soaking into the pastry to form a soggy layer at the bottom of the tart.

To bake a pastry case blind, first line it with greaseproof paper and then half fill it with ceramic baking beans. These both weight it down and help conduct the heat evenly into the pastry case during the cooking. Bake the prepared pastry case for 10-15 minutes, then remove the beans and paper and return the pastry case to the oven for a further 5-10 minutes until the base is cooked and the edges are lightly browned.

Sweet pastry cases will cook more quickly because of the sugar content. Egg in the dough will also help the pastry to keep its shape during cooking and will give a nice golden colour to the cooked case.

TART DISHES AND FRAMES

When one thinks of a tart, a round pastry usually springs to mind, but tarts can come in all manner of shapes and sizes depending on the tin or frame used. Apart from the traditional round ones, available in all sizes from very large to tiny tartlet tins, there are square, oblong and even decoratively shaped ones, such as those in the shape of a heart. All good kitchen equipment shops have a wide range of such tart tins.

Round loose-based tart tins with plain or fluted edges are the most popular as they are so easy to line with pastry. When baked, the loose base allows for easier removal of the tart from the mould.

The most popular tart tin in France is the 'tranche' (meaning 'slice'). Elongated rectangles in shape,

these come either as loose-based fluted tins or as straight-sided frames which must be placed on a baking sheet. The long narrow tarts produced by these tins need careful handling when they are being unmoulded and cut.

Individual tartlet or barquette tins are made in sizes which vary from the very tiny (2.5 cm/1 in across) up to diameters of about 15 cm/6 in and are mainly used for party or special occasion food. The larger tins come with loose bases for easier use. Ensure that rigid tins are well greased before use.

USING READY-MADE PASTRY

In this fast-moving world we often simply don't have the time to spend doing much preparation in the kitchen, so it is always helpful to use convenient shortcuts. As appropriate, ready-made frozen shortcrust and puff pastries and packet mix pastries will work well in place of the pastries I have suggested in my recipes.

As you will see, however, the pastry recipes I have given have been carefully devised to complement the filling used. Flavouring ingredients such as herbs and spices, cheeses and seasonings have been added to the savoury tarts, tartlets and barquettes to give even more mouthwatering results. Likewise the pastry cases for the sweet tarts have been enlivened with added sugar, citrus zest, nuts or chocolate to enhance their flavour.

So if you want to take advantage of bought pastries it is quite possible to add the extra flavouring ingredients to a packet pastry mix. Ready-made pastry, however, is not quite so receptive to the addition of ingredients. It is inadvisable to add sugar to it, for instance, but icing sugar may be used to dust the work surface instead of flour prior to rolling. Nuts, citrus zest, herbs and spices may also be lightly kneaded into ready-made pastry, but care must be taken not to over-knead, or the pastry will become hard and unworkable.

TARTLETS AND BARQUETTES

*I*ndividually fashioned pastry tartlets are always appealing and evocative of nursery rhymes and childhood treats, but they also have the added advantage of being easier to serve and store. Savoury versions make wonderful snacks, light lunches or starters and a selection of them may also be served to accompany drinks or as part of a buffet meal or picnic. Sweet tartlets are also excellent for lunch boxes and al fresco eating, as well as for serving with morning coffee and afternoon tea.

The French term 'barquettes' refers to boat-shaped tartlets, which are popular in haute cuisine hors d'oeuvres. Their shape makes a pleasing change and suits them particularly well to large attractive displays.

Clockwise from the top: Camembert and Cranberry Barquettes (page 12); Gruyère and Prosciutto Barquettes (page 13); a Goats' Cheese and Herb Tartlet (page 12)

When buying
Camembert cheese
for the
CAMEMBERT AND
CRANBERRY
BARQUETTES, *try
to buy a slightly
under-ripe cheese as
this will slice more
easily.*

For the GOATS'
CHEESE AND
HERB
TARTLETS, *buy a
goats' cheese which
has no flavoured
coating and is quite
soft in texture.*

PROSCIUTTO *(also
known as Parma
ham) is a traditional
Italian ham. The
pigs are fed on a diet
of whey left over
from making the
local Parmesan
cheese and the ham is
dry-cured under
weights and left to
mature for one year.
It is very thinly
sliced and served raw
as an appetizer or
used as a flavouring
in cooking.*

CAMEMBERT AND CRANBERRY BARQUETTES

MAKES 16

FOR THE PASTRY
115 g/4 oz flour
½ tsp salt
½ tsp English mustard powder
85 g/3 oz butter, cut into small pieces
1 egg yolk

FOR THE FILLING
2 tbsp orange juice
1 tbsp caster sugar
55 g/2 oz cranberries
115 g/4 oz Camembert cheese, thinly sliced

To make the pastry: sift the flour, salt and mustard powder into a bowl, add the butter and rub it in finely with the fingertips. Stir in the egg yolk and mix together with a fork to form a firm dough.

Knead the dough on a lightly floured surface until smooth. Roll it out thinly and use to line sixteen 10 cm/4 in fluted barquette moulds. Chill for 30 minutes.

Preheat the oven to 200C/400F/gas6.

Bake the pastry cases blind for 10 minutes, or until lightly browned at the edges and cooked at their bases.

While they are baking make the filling: place the orange juice, sugar and cranberries in a small saucepan. Heat gently, shaking the pan occasionally, until the cranberries are tender and the liquid has evaporated. Leave the cranberries to cool.

Arrange a little cheese in each pastry case. Just before serving, place the pastry boats in the oven for 2-3 minutes until the cheese has just melted. Remove them from the oven and arrange a few cranberries on each barquette. Serve immediately.

GOATS' CHEESE AND HERB TARTLETS*

MAKES 4

FOR THE PASTRY
115 g/4 oz flour
½ tsp salt and ¼ tsp freshly ground black pepper
85 g/3 oz butter, cut into small pieces
1 egg yolk

FOR THE FILLING
100 g/3½ oz full-fat soft goats' cheese
2 tbsp chopped mixed herbs,
including basil, marjoram and parsley
2 tbsp finely chopped spring onions
1 egg
(*see page 2 for advice on eggs)
150 ml/¼ pt single cream
½ tsp freshly ground black pepper

To make the pastry: sift the flour, salt and pepper into a bowl. Add the butter and rub it in finely with the fingertips. Stir in the egg yolk and mix together with a fork to form a firm dough.

Knead the dough on a lightly floured surface until smooth. Roll it out thinly and use to line four 11 cm/4½ in diameter loose-based fluted tart tins. Chill for 30 minutes.

Preheat the oven to 200C/400F/gas6.

Bake the cases blind for 10 minutes, or until lightly browned at the edges and cooked at their bases. Reduce the oven temperature to 190C/375F/gas5.

While they are baking make the filling: place the cheese, herbs and spring onions in a bowl and beat together until well blended. Add the egg, cream and pepper and beat again until well blended.

Pour the mixture into the pastry cases and return them to the cooler oven for 10-15 minutes, until the filling has just set. Serve warm or cold.

GRUYÈRE AND PROSCIUTTO BARQUETTES*

MAKES 6

FOR THE PASTRY
115 g/4 oz flour
½ tsp salt and ¼ tsp freshly ground pepper
85 g/3 oz butter, cut into small pieces
1 egg yolk
1 tbsp freshly chopped basil
FOR THE FILLING
85 g/3 oz Gruyère cheese, thinly sliced
55 g/2 oz prosciutto, cut into strips
150 ml/¼ pt single cream
1 egg
(* see page 2 for advice on eggs)
½ tsp French mustard
¼ tsp freshly ground pepper

To make the pastry: sift the flour, salt and pepper into a bowl, add the butter and rub it in finely with the fingertips. Stir in the egg yolk and basil and mix together with a fork to form a firm dough.

Knead the dough on a lightly floured surface until smooth. Roll it out thinly and use to line six 15 cm/6 in barquette moulds. Chill for 30 minutes.

Preheat the oven to 200C/400F/gas6.

Bake the cases blind for 10 minutes, or until lightly browned at the edges and cooked at their bases. Reduce the oven temperature to 190C/375F/gas5.

While they are baking make the filling: arrange the cheese slices in the pastry cases with the strips of prosciutto on top. In a bowl, whisk together the cream, egg, mustard and pepper.

Spoon the egg mixture into the pastry cases and return them to the cooler oven for 15 minutes, or until the filling has just set. Serve warm or cold.

QUAILS' EGGS *were once hard to find but, due to an increase in quail farming, they are now quite common and not so expensive. They are extremely fiddly to shell when cooked, so allow plenty of time if you are preparing them for a special occasion.*

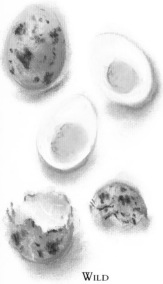

WILD MUSHROOMS, *such as chanterelles, ceps and morels, have wonderfully deep and interesting flavours and are now available widely in specialist shops and good supermarkets.*

BARQUETTES OF QUAILS' EGGS WITH CHERVIL

MAKES 20

FOR THE PASTRY
115 g/4 oz flour
85 g/3 oz butter, cut into small pieces
1 tbsp freshly grated Parmesan cheese
1 egg

FOR THE FILLING
2 egg yolks
1 tbsp raspberry vinegar
¼ tsp each salt and freshly ground black pepper
85 g/3 oz unsalted butter
½ tsp French mustard
2 tbsp chopped chervil
20 quails' eggs, hard-boiled, shelled and halved
½ tsp ground mace

To make the pastry: sift the flour into a bowl, add the butter and rub it in finely with the fingertips. Stir in the Parmesan and egg and mix to a firm dough.

Knead the dough on a lightly floured surface until smooth. Roll out thinly and use to line twenty 8.5 cm/3½ in barquette moulds. Chill for 30 minutes.

Preheat the oven to 200C/400F/gas6.

Bake the barquette cases blind for 10 minutes, until lightly browned at the edges.

While they are baking make the filling: whisk together the egg yolks, vinegar, salt and pepper.

Melt the butter over a low heat until foaming. Very gradually add the butter to the mixture while still whisking until all has been added and the mixture is creamy and thick. Stir in the mustard and chervil.

Arrange the two halves of each quails' egg in each pastry boat and carefully spoon the sauce over to cover evenly. Sprinkle lightly with the mace.

Return the pastry boats to the oven for 2-3 minutes until the sauce bubbles. Alternatively, grill them for 1 to 2 minutes. Serve immediately.

WILD MUSHROOM AND OREGANO BARQUETTES

MAKES 8

FOR THE PASTRY
115 g/4 oz flour
½ tsp salt and ¼ tsp freshly ground black pepper
85 g/3 oz butter, cut into small pieces
1 egg yolk

FOR THE FILLING
30 g/1 oz butter
2 tbsp chopped oregano
85 g/3 oz wild or oyster mushrooms
1 tbsp flour
1 tsp finely grated zest and 2 tsp juice from an unwaxed lime
1 tbsp Marsala
4 tbsp double cream
2 tbsp chopped chives
½ tsp salt and ¼ tsp freshly ground black pepper

Make the pastry: sift the flour, salt and pepper into a bowl, add the butter and rub in finely with the fingertips. Stir in the egg yolk and mix to a firm dough.

Knead the dough on a lightly floured surface until smooth. Roll it out thinly and use to line eight 10 cm/4 in barquette moulds. Chill for 30 minutes.

Preheat the oven to 200C/400F/gas6.

Bake the pastry cases blind for 10 minutes, or until lightly browned at the edges.

Melt the butter in a saucepan over a moderate heat, stir in the oregano and mushrooms and cook for 1-2 minutes. Add the flour, stir until well blended and cook for 30 seconds. Then add the lime zest and juice and the Marsala and bring to the boil, stirring. Cook for a further 1 minute, stirring continuously.

Off the heat, stir in the cream, chives, salt and pepper. Spoon into the cases and serve warm or cold.

Top: Wild Mushroom and Oregano Barquettes; bottom: Barquettes of Quails' Eggs with Chervil

PRAWN AND FENNEL TARTLETS*

MAKES 6

FOR THE PASTRY
115 g/4 oz flour
½ tsp salt and ¼ tsp freshly ground black pepper
85 g/3 oz butter, cut into small pieces
1 egg yolk
FOR THE FILLING
30 g/1 oz butter
55 g/2 oz fennel bulb, chopped
1 garlic clove, crushed
6 tbsp thick mayonnaise
2 tbsp double cream
1 egg
(* see page 2 for advice on eggs)
¼ tsp salt and ¼ tsp freshly ground black pepper
6 large peeled cooked prawns, sliced

Make the pastry: sift the flour, salt and pepper into a bowl. Add the butter and rub in finely with the fingertips. Stir in the egg yolk and mix to a firm dough.

Knead the dough on a lightly floured surface until smooth. Roll it out thinly and use to line six 8.5 cm/3½ in diameter tartlet tins. Chill for 30 minutes.

Preheat the oven to 200C/400F/gas6.

Bake the pastry cases blind for 10 minutes, or until lightly browned at the edges. Reduce the oven temperature to 190C/375F/gas5.

While they are baking make the filling: melt the butter in a heavy-based saucepan over a moderate heat, stir in the fennel and garlic and cook quickly for 1 minute. Remove the pan from the heat.

In a bowl, beat together the mayonnaise, cream, egg, salt and pepper. Stir in the fennel mixture.

Divide the prawns equally between the pastry cases and spoon over the fennel mixture.

Return the tartlets to the oven and cook for 15 minutes until the filling has just set. Serve warm or cold.

SORREL AND PIKE TARTLETS*

MAKES 6

FOR THE PASTRY
115 g/4 oz flour
½ tsp salt and ¼ tsp freshly ground black pepper
85 g/3 oz butter, cut into small pieces
1 egg yolk
FOR THE FILLING
30 g/1 oz butter
2 tbsp finely chopped spring onion
55 g/2 oz sorrel leaves, chopped
170 g/6 oz pike fillets, cut into small pieces
¼ tsp salt and ¼ tsp freshly ground black pepper
1 egg
(* see page 2 for advice on eggs)
150 ml/¼ pt single cream
1 tsp ground mace

To make the pastry: sift the flour, salt and pepper into a bowl, add the butter and rub it in finely with the fingertips. Stir in the egg yolk and mix together with a fork to form a firm dough.

Knead the dough on a lightly floured surface until smooth. Roll it out thinly and use to line six 7.5 cm/ 3 in diameter tartlet tins. Chill for 30 minutes.

Preheat the oven to 200C/400F/gas6.

Bake the pastry cases blind for 10 minutes, or until lightly browned at the edges. Reduce the oven temperature to 190C/375F/gas5.

While they are baking make the filling: melt the butter in a saucepan over a moderate heat, add the spring onions and sorrel. Cook quickly for 1 minute, stirring. Stir in the pike, salt and pepper.

Beat the egg, cream and mace together, stir in the fish mixture and spoon into the tart cases.

Return the tartlets to the oven for 15-20 minutes, until the filling has just set. Serve warm or cold.

PORT AND FIG BARQUETTES

MAKES 8

FOR THE PASTRY
115 g/4 oz flour
85 g/3 oz butter, cut into small pieces
30 g/1 oz caster sugar
1 egg yolk
FOR THE FILLING
100 ml/3½ fl oz ruby port
2 tbsp of juice and 1 tsp finely grated zest from
an unwaxed orange
2 cloves
85 g/3 oz caster sugar
4 figs
2 tsp arrowroot
150 ml/¼ pt double cream, whipped to soft peaks

Make the pastry: sift the flour into a bowl, add the butter and rub in finely with the fingertips. Stir in the sugar and egg yolk and mix to a firm dough.

Knead the dough on a lightly floured surface until smooth. Roll it out thinly and use to line eight 10 cm/4 in barquette moulds. Chill for 30 minutes.

Preheat the oven to 200C/400F/gas6.

Bake the pastry cases blind for 10 minutes, or until lightly browned at the edges. Leave to cool.

Make the filling: place the port, orange juice, orange zest, cloves and sugar in a saucepan. Heat gently, stirring occasionally, until the sugar has dissolved.

Add the figs, cover and cook gently for 4-5 minutes, until the figs are tender. Using a slotted spoon, transfer the figs to a plate and leave until cold.

Blend the arrowroot with 1 tablespoon of cold water and add to the port syrup. Bring to the boil, stirring continuously until thickened, and cook for 1 minute.

Spoon the cream into the pastry cases. Cut each fig into 6 segments and arrange 3 in each pastry case. Spoon the syrup glaze over the fruit and leave to set.

SORREL *is a soft-leaf green herb which is similar to baby spinach in appearance. It has a rich, sharp flavour and goes well with salmon. It may be made into a sauce or used to flavour soups and omelettes. Look for fresh firm leaves but do not keep them for more than 2-3 days, stored in a polythene bag in the refrigerator.*

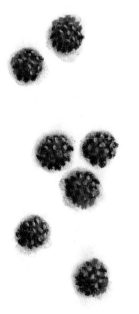

BLACKBERRY AND TANSY TARTLETS*

MAKES 6

FOR THE PASTRY
115 g/4 oz flour
85 g/3 oz butter, cut into small pieces
30 g/1 oz caster sugar
1 egg yolk

FOR THE FILLING
1 egg
(* see page 2 for advice on eggs)
75 g/2½ oz caster sugar
150 ml/¼ pt whipping cream
3 tansy or lemon geranium leaves
225 g/8 oz blackberries
2 tsp arrowroot

TANSY *is an ancient herb used mainly for its medicinal and tonic qualities. It was traditionally used to flavour cakes and custards, in sparing quantities because of its bitter flavour. Its leaves are soft and feathery and it grows in abundance, bearing bright yellow button flowers in the summer.*

To make the pastry: sift the flour into a bowl, add the butter and rub it in finely with the fingertips. Stir in the sugar and egg yolk and mix together with a fork to form a firm dough.

Knead the dough on a lightly floured surface until smooth. Roll it out thinly and use to line six 8.5 cm/3½ in heart-shaped tartlet tins. Chill for 30 minutes.

Preheat the oven to 200C/400F/gas6.

Bake the cases blind for 10 minutes, until lightly browned at the edges and cooked at their bases. Reduce the oven temperature to 160C/325F/gas3.

While they are baking make the filling: place the egg, 15 g/½ oz caster sugar and the cream in a bowl and whisk until well blended. Half fill the pastry cases with the custard and place half a tansy or lemon geranium leaf into each. Return the tartlets to the oven for 20 minutes, or until the custard has just set. Leave to cool and then remove the pieces of leaf.

While they are cooling place the blackberries and remaining sugar in a saucepan with 2 tablespoons of water. Heat gently, shaking the pan occasionally, until the blackberries are tender but still whole.

Strain the blackberries and reserve the juice, making it up to 150 ml/¼ pt with water if necessary. Blend the arrowroot with 1 tablespoon of cold water and stir it into the blackberry juice.

Return the juice to the saucepan, bring to the boil, stirring, and cook for 1 minute. Fill each tartlet with blackberries and spoon the blackberry glaze over the fruit to cover evenly. Leave to set.

BLOSSOM PINK TARTLETS*

MAKES 12

FOR THE PASTRY
200 g/7 oz flour
140 g/5 oz butter, cut into small pieces
30 g/1 oz caster sugar
1 egg, beaten

FOR THE FILLING
150 ml/¼ pt apple juice
1 tbsp caster sugar
350 g/12 oz cooking apples, peeled and thinly sliced
1 small banana, mashed
2 tsp powdered gelatine
4 tbsp sweetened condensed milk
2 tsp finely grated zest and 2 tbsp juice from an unwaxed lemon
1 egg, separated
(*see page 2 for advice on eggs)
pink food colouring

Make the pastry: sift the flour into a bowl, add the butter and rub in finely with the fingertips. Stir in the sugar and egg and mix together to form a firm dough.

Knead the dough on a lightly floured surface until smooth. Roll it out thinly and use to line twelve 7.5 cm/3 in diameter brioche moulds. Chill for 30 minutes.

Preheat the oven to 200C/400F/gas6.

Bake the tartlet cases blind for 10-15 minutes, until lightly browned at the edges and cooked at their bases. Leave to cool.

While they are baking and cooling make the filling: place the apple juice and sugar in a heavy-based saucepan, bring to the boil and add the sliced apples. Cover and cook gently for 2-3 minutes until the apple slices are tender. Using a slotted spoon, remove the apples and place them in a bowl with the banana. Mix well together and leave until cold.

Sprinkle the gelatine into the apple syrup and stir until dissolved. Leave in a cool place. Beat together the condensed milk, lemon zest, juice and egg yolk until smooth and spoon into the cases. Leave to set.

Place the egg white, apple syrup and a few drops of pink food colouring in a bowl and whisk continuously until thick and foamy.

Spoon the fruit over the custard in the cases and top with apple foam. Leave in a cool place to set.

MARSALA CREAM BARQUETTES

MAKES 8

FOR THE PASTRY
115 g/4 oz flour
85 g/3 oz butter, cut into small pieces
30 g/1 oz caster sugar
1 egg yolk
FOR THE FILLING
3 egg yolks
45 g/1½ oz flour
30 g/1 oz caster sugar
3 tbsp Marsala
150 ml/¼ pt milk
175 ml/6 fl oz double cream
85 g/3 oz plain chocolate, melted
TO DECORATE
white and dark chocolate curls

To make the pastry: sift the flour into a bowl, add the butter and rub it in finely with the fingertips. Stir in the sugar and egg yolk and mix together with a fork to form a firm dough.

Knead the dough on a lightly floured surface until smooth. Roll it out thinly and use to line eight 10 cm/4 in barquette moulds. Chill for 30 minutes.

Preheat the oven to 200C/400F/gas6.

Bake the pastry cases blind for 10 minutes, or until lightly browned at the edges and cooked at their bases.

While they are baking make the filling: place the egg yolks, flour, sugar and Marsala in a bowl and whisk together until well blended. Bring the milk to the boil in a small pan and pour it over the egg mixture, whisking continuously.

Return the custard to the saucepan and cook gently, whisking continuously until the custard thickens. Cook for 1 minute then remove the pan from the heat. Stir in the cream. Leave to cool.

Brush the insides of each pastry case with melted chocolate to coat evenly. Chill to set.

Put the cream mixture in a nylon piping bag fitted with a medium star nozzle. Pipe the filling into each pastry case.

Decorate with chocolate curls to serve.

MARSALA *is a fortified dessert wine from Sicily. A proportion of brandy is added to the local wine and part of this is heated to give it it's characteristic caramel flavour. It is used extensively in dessert recipes and is the essential flavouring for the Italian custard dessert Zabaglione.*

CHOCOLATE CURLS *are made from a block of chocolate at room temperature by shaving off small curls with a potato peeler.*

MAIDS OF HONOUR

MAKES 12

225 g/8 oz frozen puff pastry, defrosted
FOR THE FILLING
575 ml/1 pt milk
30 g/1 oz caster sugar
1 lemon geranium leaf
1 tsp rennet
30 g/1 oz butter, melted
1 egg, beaten
30 g/1 oz ground almonds
½ tsp finely grated zest from an unwaxed lemon
½ tsp ground nutmeg
1 tbsp currants
TO DECORATE
icing sugar

On a lightly floured surface, roll the pastry out to a thickness of about 3 mm/⅛ in. Using a cutter which is 1 cm/½ in greater in diameter than the tops of the tart tins being used, cut out 12 pastry rounds and use to line 12 tartlet tins. Chill until required.

Make the filling: place the milk, sugar and geranium leaf in a saucepan and heat gently until lukewarm. Remove from the heat, stir in the rennet and leave in a warm place for 5 minutes, or until thick.

Place a muslin-lined sieve over a bowl. Pour in the milk mixture and allow it to separate for at least 4 hours. Remove and discard the geranium leaf.

Preheat the oven to 220C/425F/gas7.

Place the curds, butter, egg, ground almonds, lemon zest and nutmeg in a bowl. Mix together until well blended. Spoon the mixture into the pastry cases and sprinkle them each with a few currants.

Bake in the oven for 20 minutes, until risen and lightly browned. Allow to cool in the tins for 5 minutes, then remove carefully and leave to cool on a wire rack. The tarts will sink slightly.

When cold, dust with icing sugar to decorate.

SUMMER FRUIT TARTLETS

MAKES 18

FOR THE PASTRY
115 g/4 oz flour
85 g/3 oz butter, cut into small pieces
30 g/1 oz caster sugar
1 egg yolk
FOR THE FILLING
150 ml/¼ pt double cream
1 tbsp rose water
1 tbsp icing sugar, sieved
8 tbsp apricot jam, boiled and sieved
350 g/12 oz mixed fruits, such as raspberries, redcurrants, blackcurrants and white currants, wild strawberries, seedless grapes, blueberries and sliced stoned nectarines

To make the pastry: sift the flour into a bowl, add the butter and rub it in finely with the fingertips. Stir in the sugar and egg yolk and mix together with a fork to form a firm dough.

Knead the dough on a lightly floured surface until smooth. Roll it out thinly and use to line eighteen 7.5 cm/3 in diameter fluted tartlet tins. Chill for 30 minutes.

Preheat the oven to 200C/400F/gas6.

Bake the pastry cases blind for 10 minutes, or until lightly browned at the edges and cooked at their bases. Leave to cool.

While they are baking and cooling make the filling: place the cream, rose water and icing sugar in a bowl and beat until just thick. Put in a nylon piping bag fitted with a small plain nozzle.

Brush the inside of each case with some of the sieved apricot jam and pipe a little of the cream mixture into each. Arrange the fruits on top and brush with more of the apricot glaze. Leave to set.

Top left: a heart-shaped Blackberry and Tansy Tartlet (page 18); rest of page: assorted Summer Fruit Tartlets

SAVOURY TARTS

A bout twenty years ago, the sudden vogue in this country for the French quiche marked a revival of the old-fashioned tradition of making tarts with savoury fillings. Since then all manner of imaginative variations on the theme and new inspired combinations have found their way into our repertoires. Savoury tarts work well as snacks and as lunches or light meals, with an accompanying salad. They also make useful dinner-party starters and memorable party food. Usually with a rich custard base, fillings can be as varied as the range of fresh ingredients available. Using fresh herbs and spices and exploiting the wide range of different tasty cheeses can also make interesting dishes for vegetarians.

Top: Salmon and Sorrel Tart (page 25); bottom: Asparagus and Dill Tart (page 28)

CRAB TART WITH CREAM AND BASIL

6 sheets of filo pastry
55 g/2 oz butter, melted
FOR THE FILLING *30 g/1 oz butter*
30 g/1 oz chives, finely chopped
2 tbsp finely chopped basil leaves
2 tbsp finely chopped chervil
170 g/6 oz fresh crab meat
150 ml/¼ pt sour cream
2 eggs
½ tsp salt
¼ tsp cayenne pepper
¼ tsp Tabasco sauce

Preheat the oven to 200C/400F/gas6. Brush the sheets of filo pastry generously with melted butter and arrange them in layers covering the base and sides of a 20 cm/8 in long shallow oval ovenproof dish. Tuck the overhanging excess pastry in to make a neat edge.

To make the filling: melt the butter in a saucepan, add the chives, basil and chervil and cook quickly for 1 minute, stirring.

Remove the saucepan from the heat and stir in the crab meat.

In a bowl, beat together the sour cream, eggs, salt, cayenne and Tabasco. Add this to the crab mixture and stir until well blended.

Pour the crab mixture into the pastry-lined dish, sprinkle with cayenne and bake in the oven for 20-25 minutes, until the pastry is golden brown and the filling has just set.

Serve warm or cold.

Top: Crab Tart with Cream and Basil; bottom: Mussel Tart

MUSSEL TART

SERVES 6

FOR THE PASTRY
170 g/6 oz flour
½ tsp salt
115 g/4 oz butter, cut into small pieces
1 tbsp lemon juice
FOR THE FILLING
30 g/1 oz butter
1 tbsp oil
1 onion, thinly sliced
1 garlic clove, crushed
85 g/3 oz oyster mushrooms, sliced
3 fresh bay leaves
2 tsp each chopped rosemary, thyme and parsley
12 cherry tomatoes, halved
4 tbsp white wine
150 ml/¼ pt single cream
2 eggs
½ tsp salt and ¼ tsp freshly ground black pepper
10 fresh shelled mussels, halved

Make the pastry: sift the flour and salt into a bowl, add the butter and rub in finely. Stir in the lemon juice and 2-3 tablespoons of cold water and mix to a firm dough.

Knead until smooth. Roll thinly and use to line a 23 cm/9 in pie plate. Flute the edges. Chill briefly.

Preheat the oven to 200C/400F/gas6.

Bake the pastry case blind for 10-15 minutes, until lightly browned at the edge.

Melt the butter with the oil in a pan over a moderate to high heat. Add the onion and garlic and fry for 1 minute. Add the mushrooms, herbs and tomatoes and stir for another minute. Add the wine, bring to the boil, then remove from the heat.

Beat together the cream, eggs, salt and pepper and add to the pan with the mussels. Mix well together.

Pour into the case and bake for 15-20 minutes, until set and lightly browned. Serve warm or cold.

SALMON AND SORREL TART*

SERVES 6

FOR THE PASTRY
170 g/6 oz flour
½ tsp salt and ¼ tsp freshly ground black pepper
115 g/4 oz butter, cut into small pieces
1 tbsp lemon juice
FOR THE FILLING
225 g/8 oz skinless salmon fillet, cut into small pieces
1 tbsp raspberry vinegar
1 tbsp pink peppercorns
55 g/2 oz sorrel leaves
115 g/4 oz fresh soft cheese
150 ml/¼ pt single cream
2 egg yolks
*(*see page 2 for advice on eggs)*
¼ tsp salt

To make the pastry: sift the flour, salt and pepper into a bowl, add the butter and rub it in finely with the fingertips. Stir in the lemon juice and 1-2 tablespoons of cold water and mix together to form a firm dough.

Knead until smooth. Roll thinly and use to line a 20 cm/8 in square tart tin. Chill for 30 minutes.

Preheat the oven to 200C/400F/gas6.

Bake the pastry case blind for 10-15 minutes, until lightly browned at the edges. Remove from the oven and reduce the temperature to 180C/350F/gas4.

While the case is baking make the filling: place the salmon in a bowl with the raspberry vinegar and peppercorns and leave to marinate.

Plunge the sorrel into boiling water for 1 minute. Drain and chop finely. Beat together with the cheese.

Spread the base of the pastry case with the cheese mixture. Then top this with the salmon mixture.

Beat together the cream, egg yolks and salt and pour over the salmon mixture. Return the tart to the oven for 25-30 minutes, until the filling has just set.

Cool in the tin, then remove. Serve warm or cold.

FILO, *from the Greek word for 'leaf', comprises of sheets of wafer-thin pastry. It may be used for both sweet and savoury dishes and when baked or fried has a light crisp texture. Care must be taken not to allow filo to dry out or it breaks readily, so keep it covered with a damp towel when not actually working with it.*

PINK PEPPERCORNS *are not really peppercorns at all, but a processed berry from South America.*

GARAM MASALA, *meaning hot spice mixture, is an intensely aromatic blend of ground spices used in making some Indian recipes. It is available commercially but it is possible to grind your own Garam Masala. There are many different blends, but most use coriander, cumin, cardamom, ginger, cloves and black pepper.*

The famous French tart QUICHE LORRAINE *was first made in the province of Alsace-Lorraine. Traditionally it was made with lardons of fat salt pork or green bacon set in a well-flavoured cheese custard.*

SPICED CHICKEN TART*

SERVES 6

170 g/6 oz frozen puff pastry, defrosted
FOR THE FILLING
30 g/1 oz butter or margarine
1 leek, thinly sliced
1 garlic clove, crushed
1/2 tsp ground turmeric
2 tsp ground cumin
2 tsp garam masala
225 g/8 oz chicken breast, diced
1 potato, peeled, diced and cooked
1 tbsp chopped coriander
grated zest and juice of 1 unwaxed lime
1/2 tsp salt and 1/4 tsp freshly ground black pepper
1 tbsp mango chutney
150 ml/1/4 pt single cream
2 eggs
(* see page 2 for advice on eggs)
TO GARNISH
sprigs of coriander

Roll the pastry out thinly on a lightly floured surface and use it to line a 23 cm/9 in ovenproof pie plate. Flute the edges and chill for 30 minutes.

Preheat the oven to 200C/400F/gas6.

Bake the pastry case blind for 10-15 minutes, until lightly browned at the edge.

While the case is baking make the filling: melt the butter or margarine in a saucepan over a moderate heat. Add the leek and garlic and fry quickly for 1 minute. Stir in the spices, chicken and potato. Cook, stirring frequently, until the chicken has turned white. Add the coriander, lime zest, juice, salt, pepper and chutney. Remove from the heat.

Beat together the cream and eggs and stir into the chicken mixture. Pour into the case and return to the oven for 15-20 minutes, until the filling has set.

Serve hot or cold, garnished with coriander.

QUICHE LORRAINE*

SERVES 6

FOR THE PASTRY
170 g/6 oz flour
1/2 tsp salt
115 g/4 oz butter, cut into small pieces
1 tbsp lemon juice
FOR THE FILLING
115 g/4 oz unsmoked bacon, grilled and finely chopped
170 g/6 oz Gruyère cheese, grated
4 egg yolks
(* see page 2 for advice on eggs)
300 ml/1/2 pt single cream
1 tsp freshly grated nutmeg
1/4 tsp freshly ground black pepper
1 tsp French mustard

Make the pastry: sift the flour and salt into a bowl, add the butter and rub it in finely with the fingertips. Stir in the lemon juice and 2 tablespoons of cold water and mix to a firm dough.

Knead the dough on a lightly floured surface until smooth. Roll it out thinly and use to line a 23 cm/9 in diameter loose-based fluted tart tin. Chill for 30 minutes.

Preheat the oven to 200C/400F/gas6.

Bake the pastry case blind for 10-15 minutes, until lightly browned at the edge. Reduce the oven temperature to 180C/350F/gas4.

While the case is baking make the filling: scatter the bacon and cheese over the pastry case.

In a bowl, beat together the egg yolks, cream, nutmeg, pepper and mustard until well blended.

Pour into the case, return it to the oven and cook for 25-30 minutes, until the filling has just set.

Cool in the tin, remove and serve warm or cold.

Top: Spiced Chicken Tart; bottom: Chicken Liver and Redcurrant Tart (page 28)

CHICKEN LIVER AND REDCURRANT TART*

FOR THE PASTRY
85 g/3 oz plain wholemeal flour
85 g/3 oz flour
85 g/3 oz butter or margarine, cut into small pieces
1 tsp chopped rosemary
FOR THE FILLING
30 g/1 oz butter
3 spring onions, thinly sliced
1 garlic clove, crushed
2 tsp chopped rosemary
170 g/6 oz chicken livers, chopped
2 tbsp Marsala
4 tbsp sour cream
1 egg
(see page 2 for advice on eggs)*
½ tsp salt and ¼ tsp freshly ground black pepper
55 g/2 oz redcurrants
TO GARNISH
sprigs of rosemary

To make the pastry: sift the flours into a bowl, add the butter or margarine and rub it in finely with the fingertips. Stir in the rosemary and 3-4 tablespoons of cold water and mix together with a fork to form a firm dough.

Knead on a lightly floured surface until smooth. Roll it out thinly and use to line a 35 x 10 cm/14 x 4 in loose-based tart tin. Chill for 30 minutes.

Preheat the oven to 200C/400F/gas6.

Bake the pastry case blind for 10-15 minutes, until lightly browned at the edges.

While the case is baking make the filling: melt the butter in a frying pan over a moderate to high heat, add the spring onions, garlic and rosemary and fry quickly for 1 minute. Add the chicken livers and fry for 1-2 minutes, until browned. Stir in the Marsala and remove from the heat.

In a bowl, beat together the sour cream, egg, salt and pepper. Add this to the liver mixture and stir gently until well blended. Reserving a whole strand of redcurrants, remove the remaining stalks and add the redcurrants to the liver mixture.

Pour the mixture into the pastry case and level the top. Return it to the oven and bake for 15-20 minutes, until the filling has just set.

Leave to cool in the tin for 5 minutes, then remove carefully. Serve hot or cold, garnished with sprigs of rosemary and the reserved redcurrants.

ASPARAGUS AND DILL TART*

SERVES 6

FOR THE PASTRY
170 g/6 oz flour
½ tsp salt and ¼ tsp freshly ground black pepper
¼ tsp mustard powder
85 g/3 oz butter or margarine, cut into small pieces
55 g/2 oz Cheddar cheese, finely grated
1 egg yolk
FOR THE FILLING
170 g/6 oz asparagus tips
1 egg + 1 extra yolk
*(*see page 2 for advice on eggs)*
300 ml/½ pt single cream
½ tsp salt and ¼ tsp finely ground black pepper
3 tbsp chopped dill
2 tsp French mustard

To make the pastry: sift the flour, salt, pepper and mustard powder into a bowl, add the butter or margarine and rub it in finely with the fingertips. Stir in the cheese, egg yolk and 1-2 tablespoons of cold water and mix together to a firm dough.

Knead the dough on a lightly floured surface until smooth. Roll it out thinly and use to line a 35 x

10 cm/14 x 4 in loose-based tranche tart tin. Chill for 30 minutes.

Preheat the oven to 200C/400F/gas6.

Bake the pastry case blind for 10-15 minutes, until lightly browned at the edges and cooked at the base. Reduce the oven temperature to 180/350F/gas4.

While the case is baking make the filling: cook the asparagus in boiling water for 1 minute, then drain well. In a bowl beat together the egg and extra egg yolk, cream, salt, pepper, dill and mustard until well blended. Pour this filling into the pastry case and arrange the asparagus tips over it.

Return to the cooler oven and bake for 20-25 minutes, until the filling has just set.

Allow to cool in the tin, then remove carefully and serve warm or cold.

SPINACH AND RAISIN TART*

FOR THE PASTRY
115 g/4 oz flour
½ tsp salt
55 g/2 oz butter or margarine, cut into small pieces
1 tbsp lemon juice
FOR THE FILLING
225 g/8 oz fresh spinach
2 eggs
*(*see page 2 for advice on eggs)*
200 ml/7 fl oz Greek yogurt
½ tsp salt and ¼ tsp finely ground black pepper
1 tsp freshly grated nutmeg
55 g/2 oz raisins

To make the pastry: sift the flour and salt into a bowl, add the butter or margarine and rub it in finely with the fingertips. Stir in the lemon juice and 2-3 tablespoons of cold water and mix together with a fork to form a firm dough.

Knead on a lightly floured surface until smooth. Roll it out thinly and use to line a 20 cm/8 in diameter loose-based fluted tart tin. Chill for 30 minutes.

Preheat the oven to 200C/400F/gas6.

Bake the pastry case blind for 10-15 minutes, until lightly browned at the edge and cooked at the base. Remove from the oven, and reduce the oven temperature to 180C/350F/gas4.

While the case is baking, make the filling: plunge the spinach into a saucepan of boiling water for 1 minute. Drain well and chop finely.

Place the eggs, yogurt, salt, pepper and nutmeg in a bowl and beat them together until well blended. Stir in the spinach and raisins and pour the mixture into the pastry case. Return the tart to the cooler oven for 20-25 minutes, until the filling has set.

Leave to cool in the tin, then remove it carefully. Serve warm or cold.

ASPARAGUS is now available throughout the year, although its true season is from June to July. When buying asparagus, look for tightly closed 'buds' or tips and fresh green unwrinkled stems. Nowadays, ready-trimmed tips are available from supermarkets, but you can use the stems for soups and sauces.

FRESH HERB AND GARLIC TART*

FOR THE PASTRY
115 g/4 oz flour
1 tbsp Parmesan cheese
¼ tsp mustard powder
½ tsp salt and ¼ tsp freshly ground black pepper
55 g/2 oz butter or margarine, cut into small pieces

FOR THE FILLING
2 garlic cloves, crushed
4 tbsp chopped mixed herbs, including parsley, rosemary,
oregano and basil
115 g/4 oz medium-fat soft cheese
4 tbsp Greek yogurt
2 eggs, beaten
(*see page 2 for advice on eggs)
½ tsp salt and ¼ tsp freshly ground black pepper

To make the pastry: sift the flour, Parmesan, mustard, salt and pepper into a bowl. Add the margarine or butter and rub it in finely with the fingertips. Stir in 2-3 tablespoons of cold water and mix together with a fork to form a firm dough.

Knead on a lightly floured surface until smooth. Roll out thinly and use to line a 20 cm/8 in diameter loose-based tart tin. Chill for 30 minutes.

Preheat the oven to 200C/400F/gas6.

Bake the case blind for 10-15 minutes, until lightly browned at the edge and cooked at the base. Reduce the oven temperature to 180C/350F/gas4.

While the case is baking make the filling: mix the garlic, herbs and soft cheese together in a bowl until well blended. Stir in the yogurt, eggs, salt and pepper and mix well.

Pour the mixture into the pastry case and return it to the cooler oven for 20-25 minutes, until the filling has set. Serve warm or cold.

ONION AND SAGE TART*

SERVES 6

FOR THE PASTRY
170 g/6 oz flour
½ tsp salt
55 g/2 oz white fat, cut into small pieces
55 g/2 oz butter or margarine, cut into small pieces

FOR THE FILLING
350 g/12 oz tiny onions, unpeeled
30 g/1 oz butter
15 cherry tomatoes
2 tbsp chopped sage
1 tbsp flour
150 ml/¼ pt vegetable stock
100 ml/3½ fl oz single cream
2 eggs, beaten
(*see page 2 for advice on eggs)
½ tsp salt and ¼ tsp freshly ground black pepper

FOR THE TOPPING
1 tbsp freshly grated Parmesan cheese
1 tbsp chopped sage

To make the pastry: sift the flour and salt into a bowl, add the white fat and butter or margarine and rub them in finely with the fingertips. Stir in 2 table-spoons of cold water and mix together with a fork to form a firm dough.

Knead the dough on a lightly floured surface until smooth. Roll it out thinly and use to line a 23 cm/9 in diameter loose-based tart tin. Chill for 30 minutes.

Preheat the oven to 200C/400F/gas6.

Bake the pastry case blind for 10-15 minutes, until lightly browned at the edge and cooked in the base.

While the case is baking make the filling: place the onions in a saucepan and cover with cold water. Bring to the boil, cover and cook for 10 minutes, until tender. Drain and cover with cold water. Drain again and then peel off the onion skins.

Melt the butter in a saucepan over a moderate to high heat. Add the peeled onions, the tomatoes and sage and cook quickly for 1-2 minutes, shaking the saucepan continuously. Using a slotted spoon, transfer the tomatoes and onions to a plate. Allow to cool slightly then cut them in half. Arrange them in the pastry case.

Add the flour to the juices in the saucepan and stir well. Add the vegetable stock, bring to the boil and cook for 1 minute. Remove the saucepan from the heat, stir in the cream, eggs, salt and pepper.

Pour the mixture into the pastry case and return it to the oven for 15 minutes. Remove from the oven and give the tart its topping: sprinkle the top with Parmesan cheese and sage and continue to cook for a further 10-15 minutes, until the filling has set and is golden brown. Serve hot or cold.

Left: Fresh Herb and Garlic Tart; right: Onion and Sage Tart

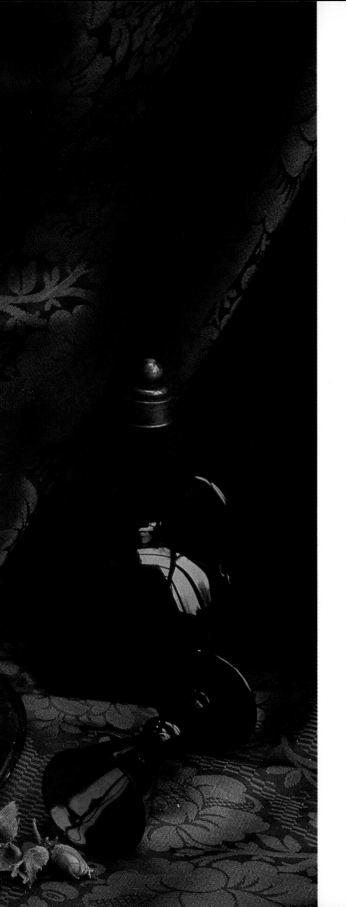

TRADITIONAL COUNTRY TARTS

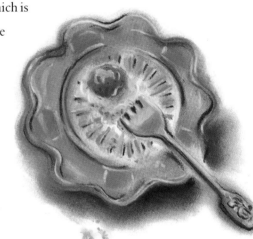

Many regions have their own very particular time-honoured tart recipes which have been passed down from generation to generation. Some, like the Bakewell Tart or the Yorkshire Curd Tart, are so delicious that they soon became firm favourites all over the country and even in other parts of the world. However, some of the recipes I have produced for this chapter are my own very special adaptations of old favourites, like the Kentish Strawberry Tart which is based on the strawberry trifle traditional in that part of the world, or the Highland Tart which incorporates the popular Scottish oatmeal dessert Atholl Brose.

Left: Mincemeat and Orange Tart (page 34); right: Highland Tart (page 34)

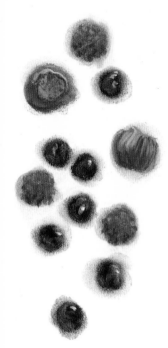

HIGHLAND TART

SERVES 6

FOR THE PASTRY
115 g/4 oz flour
30 g/1 oz hazelnuts, toasted and finely chopped
85 g/3 oz butter or margarine, cut into small pieces
30 g/1 oz caster sugar
1 egg yolk
FOR THE FILLING
250 ml/8 fl oz double cream
3-4 tbsp whisky
2 tbsp clear honey
55 g/2 oz medium oatmeal, toasted
170 g/6 oz mixed golden and red raspberries
170 g/6 oz blueberries
3 tbsp quince jelly, melted

To make the pastry: sift the flour into a bowl, stir in the hazelnuts, add the butter or margarine and rub it in finely with the fingertips. Stir in the sugar, egg yolk and 1 tablespoon of cold water and mix together with a fork to form a firm dough.

Knead the dough on a lightly floured surface until smooth. Roll it out thinly and use to line a 20 cm/ 8 in diameter loose-based fluted tart tin. Chill for 30 minutes.

Preheat the oven to 200C/400F/gas6.

Bake the pastry case blind for 15-20 minutes, until lightly browned at the edge and cooked at the base.

While the case is cooling make the filling: place the cream, whisky and honey in a bowl and whisk together until they are the consistency of thick cream. Fold in the oatmeal until evenly mixed.

Spread the oatmeal mixture over the base of the pastry case and arrange the fruit over the top. Brush the fruit with the quince jelly glaze and leave to set.

MINCEMEAT AND ORANGE TART

SERVES 6

FOR THE PASTRY
170 g/6 oz flour
85 g/3 oz butter, cut into small pieces
30 g/1 oz caster sugar
2 tsp finely grated zest from an unwaxed orange
FOR THE FILLING
8 tbsp mincemeat
2 unwaxed seedless oranges
170 g/6 oz caster sugar
2 tbsp Grand Marnier or Cointreau

To make the pastry: sift the flour into a bowl, add the butter and rub it in finely with the fingertips. Stir in the sugar, orange zest and 2-3 tablespoons of cold water and mix together to a firm dough.

Knead the dough on a lightly floured surface until smooth. Roll it out thinly and use to line a 36 x 10 cm/14 x 4 in tranche frame on a baking sheet. Chill for 30 minutes.

Preheat the oven to 200C/400F/gas6.

To make the filling: spread the mincemeat evenly into the pastry case and bake in the oven for 30-35 minutes, until the pastry is golden brown.

Meanwhile, plunge the oranges into boiling water for 1 minute to blanch the skins. Allow to cool and then slice thinly.

Put the sugar in a frying pan with 250 ml/8 fl oz of water and stir until the sugar has dissolved. Add the orange slices and simmer gently for 15-20 minutes, until the rind is tender and translucent.

Remove the orange slices using a slotted spoon, cut the slices in half and arrange them over the mincemeat filling. Sprinkle over the liqueur.

Boil the juice remaining in the pan for 2-3 minutes, until it becomes syrupy. Spoon the syrup over the oranges to glaze. Leave to cool.

HARLEQUIN TART

SERVES 6

FOR THE PASTRY
200 g/7 oz flour
115 g/4 oz butter or margarine, cut into small pieces
1 tbsp caster sugar
FOR THE FILLING
6 tbsp apricot conserve
6 tbsp lemon and lime marmalade
6 tbsp raspberry conserve

To make the pastry: sift the flour into a bowl, add the margarine or butter and rub it in finely with the fingertips. Stir in the sugar and 3-4 tablespoons of cold water and mix together with a fork to form a firm dough.

Knead the dough on a lightly floured surface until smooth. Roll it out thinly and use to line a 20 cm/ 8 in square loose-based fluted tart tin, reserving the pastry trimmings. Chill for 30 minutes.

Preheat the oven to 200C/400F/gas6.

Using a skewer or cocktail stick, lightly mark on the base of the pastry case two diagonal lines connecting opposite corners. Then mark another two lines joining the mid-points of opposite edges of the pastry case, dividing the pastry case into 8 triangles. Mark 4 more lines across the corners of the pastry case, connecting mid-points of adjacent sides, to form 16 triangles in all.

Carefully fill each triangle with one of the jams or the marmalade, alternating the colours and flavours. Spread each layer evenly.

Knead the pastry trimmings together and roll out to a thin oblong. Cut out into thin strips and lay the strips across the tart to separate the jam triangles. Trim all the strips to fit.

Bake in the oven for 15-20 minutes, until the pastry is pale golden in colour. Serve warm or cold.

If the jams in the HARLEQUIN TART *recipe are not available, simply use a mixture of different coloured jams such as strawberry, plum, greengage, cherry and lemon curd.*

Harlequin Tart

MALVERN TART is a recipe devised from Malvern Pudding, a dish which originated in Worcestershire. A sweet sauce was topped with sugar and spices and then baked until golden. Apples, being plentiful in the Malvern area, were added to the recipe to give a variation.

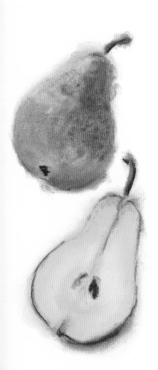

MALVERN TART

SERVES 6

FOR THE PASTRY

170 g/6 oz flour
115 g/4 oz butter or margarine, cut into small pieces
30 g/1 oz caster sugar
1 egg yolk

FOR THE FILLING

55 g/2 oz butter
55 g/2 oz caster sugar
4 dessert pears, peeled and thinly sliced
1 quince, peeled and thinly sliced
30 g/1 oz flour
450 ml/¾ pt milk
1 bay leaf

FOR THE TOPPING

55 g/2 oz demerara sugar
½ tsp ground cinnamon

To make the pastry: sift the flour into a bowl, add the butter or margarine and rub it in finely with the fingertips. Stir in the sugar, egg yolk and 2-3 tablespoons of cold water and mix together with a fork to form a firm dough.

Knead on a lightly floured surface until smooth. Roll it out thinly and use to line a 23 cm/9 in diameter ovenproof tart dish. Chill for 30 minutes.

Preheat the oven to 200C/400F/gas6.

Bake the pastry case blind for 15-20 minutes, until lightly browned and cooked at the base.

While the case is baking make the filling: melt half the butter with half the sugar in a saucepan over a moderate heat. Add the pears and quince and cook rapidly, stirring occasionally, until the fruit is tender and the juice has turned syrupy. Pour the contents of the pan into the pastry case.

Place the remaining butter and sugar and the flour, milk and bay leaf in the pan. Whisk together continuously over a moderate heat and bring to the boil. Cook gently for 1-2 minutes, until the sauce is thick and smooth. Remove the bay leaf and pour the sauce over the fruit in the pastry case. Allow to cool so that the sauce sets on top.

To make the tart topping: preheat a hot grill and mix together the demerara sugar and cinnamon. Sprinkle this over the tart filling and grill until the sugar has caramelized. Serve hot or cold.

DUKE OF CAMBRIDGE TART

FOR THE PASTRY

115 g/4 oz flour
55 g/2 oz margarine, cut into small pieces
2 tsp caster sugar
2-3 tbsp lemon juice

FOR THE FILLING

2 tbsp quince jelly
finely grated zest and 1 tbsp juice from an unwaxed lemon
1 tbsp mixed cut peel
115 g/4 oz mixed glacé fruits, chopped
55 g/2 oz self-raising flour
½ tsp baking powder
55 g/2 oz caster sugar
55 g/2 oz soft margarine
1 egg

TO DECORATE

icing sugar

To make the pastry: sift the flour, add the margarine and rub it in finely with the fingertips. Stir in the sugar and lemon juice and mix together with a fork to form a firm dough.

Knead the dough on a lightly floured surface until smooth. Roll it out thinly and use to line a 20 cm/ 8 in diameter ovenproof tart plate. Chill for about 30 minutes.

Preheat the oven to 160C/325F/gas3.

Duke of Cambridge Tart

To make the filling: spread the quince jelly over the base of the pastry case. In a bowl mix together the lemon zest, mixed peel and two-thirds of the chopped mixed glacé fruits.

Sift the flour and baking powder into a bowl. Add the sugar, margarine and egg. Mix together with a wooden spoon and beat for 1-2 minutes, until light and fluffy. Stir in the mixed fruit until well blended. Spread the filling evenly over the bottom of the pastry case.

Bake in the oven for 40-45 minutes until the filling is well risen, golden brown and firm to the touch in the centre.

Dust the top with icing sugar and decorate with the remaining chopped mixed glacé fruits. Serve hot, warm or cold.

NORFOLK TREACLE TART

SERVES 8

FOR THE PASTRY
170 g/6 oz flour
115 g/4 oz butter, cut into small pieces
1 tbsp lemon juice
FOR THE FILLING
225 g/8 oz golden syrup
30 g/1 oz butter
6 tbsp single cream
2 eggs, beaten
grated zest and juice from 1 unwaxed lemon
55 g/2 oz white breadcrumbs

To make the pastry: sift the flour into a bowl, add the butter and rub it in finely with the fingertips. Stir in the lemon juice and 2 tablespoons of cold water and mix together with a fork to form a firm dough.

Knead the dough on a lightly floured surface until smooth. Roll it out thinly and use to line a 23 cm/ 9 in diameter ovenproof tart plate, reserving the pastry trimmings. Chill for 30 minutes.

Preheat the oven to 200C/400F/gas6.

To make the filling: place the golden syrup in a saucepan and heat gently until just melted. Remove the pan from the heat, add the butter and stir until melted. Then beat in the cream, eggs, lemon zest and juice until well blended.

Sprinkle the breadcrumbs over the pastry case and pour the mixture over the top. Roll out the pastry trimmings, cut them into thin strips and use to make a lattice design over the top.

Bake in the oven for 40-45 minutes, until the pastry is golden brown and the filling has set. Allow to cool in the dish and serve warm or cold.

Clockwise from the top: Fruit Bakewell Tart; Rum and Butterscotch Tart (page 40); Norfolk Treacle Tart

FRUIT BAKEWELL TART

SERVES 6

FOR THE PASTRY
115 g/4 oz flour
55 g/2 oz margarine, cut into small pieces
1 tsp caster sugar
FOR THE FILLING
3 tbsp redcurrant jelly
*85 g/3 oz each redcurrants, white currants
and blackcurrants*
85 g/3 oz soft margarine
85 g/3 oz caster sugar
55 g/2 oz ground almonds
55 g/2 oz self-raising flour
2 eggs, beaten
1 tsp almond essence
30 g/1 oz flaked almonds
TO DECORATE
icing sugar

To make the pastry: sift the flour into a bowl, add the margarine and rub it in finely. Stir in the sugar and 2 tablespoons of cold water and mix to a firm dough.

Knead the dough until smooth. Roll out thinly and use to line a 20 cm/8 in diameter loose-based fluted tart tin. Chill for 30 minutes.

Preheat the oven to 180C/350F/gas4.

To make the filling: spread the redcurrant jelly over the base of the case. Reserve a few strands of each type of fruit for decoration, and remove the remainder from their stalks. Scatter over the jelly.

Beat together the margarine, sugar, almonds, flour, eggs and almond essence for 1-2 minutes.

Spread this mixture over the fruit in the pastry case. Scatter the flaked almonds evenly over the top and bake for 45-50 minutes, until the sponge has risen and feels firm when pressed lightly in the centre.

Cool in the tin, then remove carefully. Dust with icing sugar and decorate with the reserved fruit.

BAKEWELL TART, *or pudding as it was sometimes called, is named after the town of Bakewell in Derbyshire. The layers were traditionally separated by crushed raspberries or raspberry conserve, to add moisture.*

TREACLE TART *is said to have originated in Essex. The Norfolk variety introduced eggs, cream and lemon.*

KENTISH
STRAWBERRY
TART *is named after
the Kentish
strawberry trifle
which is used in this
recipe, enclosed in a
light crisp almond
pastry. Trifles were
very popular in
Victorian England.
They were made
using light sponge
cakes soaked in
sherry, brandy or
Madeira, layered
with fruit – Kentish
strawberries being
the most popular –
and covered with a
rich egg custard.*

RUM AND BUTTERSCOTCH TART

SERVES 6

FOR THE PASTRY
170 g/6 oz flour
115 g/4 oz butter
30 g/1 oz caster sugar
1 egg
FOR THE FILLING
115 g/4 oz soft dark brown sugar
55 g/2 oz butter
45 g/1½ oz flour
300 ml/½ pt milk
150 ml/¼ pt single cream
2-3 tbsp dark rum
TO DECORATE
4 tbsp whipped cream
chocolate coffee beans

To make the pastry: sift the flour into a bowl, add the butter and rub it in finely with the fingertips. Stir in the sugar and egg and mix together with a fork to form a firm dough.

Knead the dough on a lightly floured surface until smooth. Roll it out thinly and use to line a 23 cm/ 9 in diameter ovenproof tart dish. Chill for 30 minutes.

Preheat the oven to 200C/400F/gas6.

Bake the pastry case blind for 15-20 minutes, until lightly browned at the edge and cooked at the base.

While the case is cooling make the filling: place the sugar, butter, flour, milk and cream in a saucepan. Whisk together continuously over a moderate heat and bring to the boil. Cook gently for 1-2 minutes, until the sauce is thick and smooth. Stir in the rum.

Pour the filling into the pastry case and leave until cold. Decorate the top with whipped cream and the chocolate coffee beans.

KENTISH STRAWBERRY TART

SERVES 8

FOR THE PASTRY
115 g/4 oz flour
55 g/2 oz ground almonds
115 g/4 oz butter, cut into small pieces
30 g/1 oz caster sugar
1 tsp almond essence
1 egg
FOR THE FILLING
1 egg + 1 extra yolk
1 tsp vanilla essence
30 g/1 oz caster sugar
30 g/1 oz flour
300 ml/½ pt milk
3 tbsp strawberry jam
10 sponge fingers, cut into halves
2 tbsp Madeira
225 g/8 oz strawberries, sliced
300 ml/½ pt double cream, whipped
TO DECORATE
strawberry slices and strawberry leaves

Make the pastry: sift the flour into a bowl, stir in the almonds, add the butter and rub in finely. Stir in the sugar, almond essence and egg and mix to a firm dough.

Knead the dough until smooth. Roll it out thinly and use to line a 27.5 x 17.5 cm/11 x 7 in oblong ovenproof fluted tart dish. Chill for 30 minutes.

Preheat the oven to 200C/400F/gas6.

Bake the pastry case blind for 15-20 minutes, until lightly browned at the edges.

While the case is baking, make the filling: in a bowl whisk together the egg, egg yolk, vanilla essence, sugar and flour until well blended. Place the milk in a saucepan and bring it to the boil. Whisking continuously, pour the milk over the egg mixture. Return to the pan and continue whisking over a low heat until the custard thickens. Allow to cool.

Spread the pastry case with jam. Dip the sponge fingers into the Madeira, turning to coat well. Arrange them over the jam. Cover with strawberry slices.

Fold two-thirds of the whipped cream into the custard and spread evenly over the strawberries.

Place the remaining cream in a piping bag fitted with a small star nozzle. Pipe ropes of cream across the tart and decorate with strawberry slices and leaves.

IRISH APPLE TART

SERVES 6

FOR THE PASTRY
85 g/3 oz flour
30 g/1 oz butter, cut into small pieces
1 tsp caster sugar
225 g/8 oz floury potatoes, cooked and sieved
FOR THE FILLING
675 g/1½ lb apples, thinly sliced
30 g/1 oz caster sugar
1 tsp ground cloves
150 ml/¼ pt sour cream
2 tsp clear honey

To make the pastry: place the flour in a bowl, add the butter and rub it in finely with the fingertips. Stir in the sugar and potato and mix to a soft dough.

Roll the dough out thinly and use to line a 23 cm/9 in diameter ovenproof tart plate.

Preheat the oven to 190C/375F/gas5.

Mix together the apples, sugar and cloves and pile the mixture into the pastry case. Bake for 20-25 minutes, or until the apples are almost tender.

Stir the apples, spread the sour cream over the top and drizzle with honey. Bake for a further 5-10 minutes, until the cream has set. Serve warm or cold.

Kentish Strawberry Tart

FRUIT TARTS

*F*ruit tarts are among the most popular and eye-catching of pastries. They make one of the most appealing ways of serving the bounties of the summer fruit season and are usually fairly simple items where only the pastry case is baked. Often with no more than a layer of custard or flavoured cream beneath the fruit, they are usually finished with a coating of fruit glaze over the fruit to hold it in place and help keep it fresh.

The French often make their fruit tarts in the long rectangular 'tranche' frame, so called because the finished pastry then lends itself to being sliced across into rectangular pieces for easier serving.

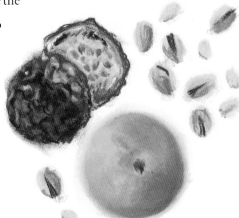

Chopped nuts, tiny mint sprigs or a light dusting of icing sugar are the most usual decorations.

Clockwise from the top: Peach and Passion Tart (page 44); Plum and Sour Cream Tart (page 44); Minted Currant Tart (page 45)

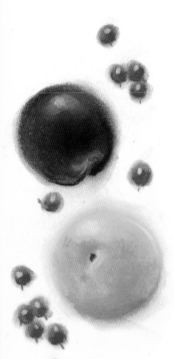

PLUM AND SOUR CREAM TART

SERVES 6

FOR THE PASTRY
170 g/6 oz flour
115 g/4 oz butter, cut into small pieces
30 g/1 oz caster sugar
3 tbsp sour cream
FOR THE FILLING
55 g/2 oz amaretti biscuits, crushed
4 tbsp sour cream
55 g/2 oz light soft brown sugar
225 g/8 oz red plums, halved
225 g/8 oz yellow plums, halved
4 tbsp redcurrant jelly

To make the pastry: sift the flour into a bowl, add the butter and rub it in finely with the fingertips. Stir in the sugar and sour cream and mix together with a fork to form a firm dough.

Knead the dough on a lightly floured surface until it is smooth. Roll it out thinly and use to line a 20 cm/8 in diameter loose-based fluted tart tin, reserving the trimmings. Chill for 30 minutes.

Preheat the oven to 190C/375F/gas5.

To make the filling: in a bowl, mix together the crushed biscuits, sour cream and brown sugar. Spread the mixture over the pastry case and arrange the plums on top, alternating the colours.

Roll out the pastry trimmings thinly and cut out 12 thin strips. Arrange these over the plums in a lattice design. Trim off the ends and press the strips on to the edge of the pastry case.

Bake in the oven for 35-40 minutes, or until the pastry is lightly browned and the plums are tender. Leave to cool.

Heat the redcurrant jelly until melted, then pour it in between the pastry lattice to glaze the tart. Leave to set.

PEACH AND PASSION TART

SERVES 8

FOR THE PASTRY
170 g/6 oz flour
115 g/4 oz butter, cut into small pieces
30 g/1 oz caster sugar
1 egg
FOR THE FILLING
2 eggs
100 ml/3½ fl oz double cream
55 g/2 oz caster sugar
strained juice from 3 passion fruit
6 peaches, skinned and halved
30 g/1 oz pistachio nuts, shelled
4 tbsp apricot jam, boiled and sieved

To make the pastry: sift the flour into a bowl, add the butter and rub it in finely with the fingertips. Stir in the caster sugar and egg and mix together with a fork to form a firm dough.

Knead the dough on a lightly floured surface until it is smooth. Roll it out thinly and use to line a 23 cm/9 in diameter ovenproof tart dish. Chill for 30 minutes.

Preheat the oven to 200C/400F/gas6.

Bake the chilled pastry case blind for 10-15 minutes, until lightly browned at the edge and cooked at the base. Reduce the oven temperature to 160C/325F/gas3.

While the case is baking make the filling: place the eggs, cream, sugar and passion fruit juice into a bowl. Beat together until well blended.

Pour the mixture into the pastry case and return it to the oven for 30-40 minutes, until the custard has set. Leave to cool.

Arrange the peaches over the custard filling and decorate with pistachio nuts. Brush the top with the apricot jam glaze and leave to set.

MINTED CURRANT TART

SERVES 6

FOR THE PASTRY
115 g/4 oz flour
85 g/3 oz butter, cut into small pieces
30 g/1 oz caster sugar
1 egg yolk
FOR THE FILLING
350 g/12 oz redcurrants
350 g/12 oz white currants
2 sprigs of mint
4 tbsp cornflour
115 g/4 oz caster sugar
TO DECORATE
sprigs of mint

To make the pastry: sift the flour into a bowl, add the butter and rub in finely with the fingertips. Stir in the sugar and egg yolk and mix to a firm dough.

Knead the dough until it is smooth. Roll it out thinly and use to line a 20 cm/8 in diameter loose-based fluted tart tin. Chill for 30 minutes.

Preheat the oven to 200C/400F/gas6.

Bake the pastry case blind for 15-20 minutes, until lightly browned at the edge.

While the case is baking make the filling: place half each of the redcurrants and white currants together with the mint in a saucepan with 250 ml/8 fl oz of water. Bring to the boil and cook for 2 minutes. Pour the contents of the saucepan into a sieve over a bowl and rub through the fruit, discarding the stems and pips.

Blend the cornflour with 4 tablespoons of water in a saucepan. Add the strained fruit purée, stir well and bring to the boil. Allow to cool for 5 minutes, stir in the sugar and pour the mixture into the pastry case. Leave until cold.

Decorate the top of the tart with the remaining redcurrants and white currants and fresh mint sprigs.

TARTE FRANÇAISE

SERVES 8

375 g/13 oz frozen puff pastry, defrosted
FOR THE FILLING
6 tbsp apricot jam, boiled and sieved
170 g/6 oz full-fat cream cheese
3 tbsp plain natural yogurt
3 tsp clear honey
1 tsp vanilla essence
450 g/1 lb mixed soft fruits, such as cherries, raspberries,
strawberries, apricots, peaches, plums, stoned and sliced
as necessary

Roll the pastry out on a lightly floured surface to make an oblong about 30 x 20 cm/12 x 8 in. Lightly flour the pastry surface and then fold the pastry in half lengthwise to make a long narrow oblong.

Measure 2.5 cm/1 in down from the top of one narrow edge and cut across the fold to within 2.5 cm/1 in of the open edge. Repeat at the bottom.

Cut a line 2.5 cm/1 in in from the open edge to join up with the side cuts. Remove the centre piece from the 'frame', open out the pastry and roll out and trim to match the size of the pastry 'frame'.

Place the oblong on a wetted baking sheet, brush the edges with water and place the frame on top. Press the edges together to seal well. Cut up the edges with a knife to form flakes. Mark a design on the top of the edges. Prick the base and chill for 30 minutes.

Meanwhile, preheat the oven to 220C/425F/gas7.

Bake the pastry case for 15-20 minutes, until risen and golden brown. Allow to cool on a wire rack and brush the base with some of the apricot jam glaze.

Beat the cream cheese, yogurt, honey and vanilla essence together in a bowl until well blended. Spread the mixture evenly over the base of the pastry tart and cover with an arrangement of soft fruits. Brush well with the remaining glaze and leave to set.

Citrus Tart

KUMQUAT FRANGIPANE TART

SERVES 6

FOR THE PASTRY
115 g/4 oz flour
85 g/3 oz butter, cut into small pieces
30 g/1 oz caster sugar
1 egg yolk
FOR THE FILLING
85 g/3 oz butter, softened
255 g/9 oz caster sugar
1 egg + 1 extra yolk
85 g/3 oz ground almonds
1 tbsp cornflour
1 tsp almond essence
4 tbsp apricot jam
170 g/6 oz kumquats, sliced

To make the pastry: sift the flour into a bowl, add the butter and rub it in finely with the fingertips. Stir in the sugar and egg yolk and mix together with a fork to form a firm dough.

Knead the dough lightly on a floured surface until it is smooth. Roll it out thinly and use to line a 36 x 10 cm/14 x 4 in loose-based fluted tranche tin. Chill for 30 minutes.

Preheat the oven to 200C/400F/gas6.

Bake the pastry case blind for 10 minutes, until lightly browned at the edges and cooked at the base. Reduce the oven temperature to 180C/350F/gas4.

While the case is baking make the filling: place the butter and 85 g/3 oz of the sugar in a bowl and beat them together with a wooden spoon until light and fluffy. Gradually add the egg and egg yolk, beating well after each addition. Fold in the ground almonds, cornflour and almond essence until evenly mixed.

Spread the base of the pastry case with the apricot

jam and place the almond mixture on top, spreading it evenly. Bake in the cooler oven for 45-50 minutes, until the filling is well risen, golden brown and firm to the touch in the centre. Leave to cool slightly before removing it from the tin.

Place the remaining sugar and 250 ml/8 fl oz of water in a saucepan and heat gently, stirring occasionally until the sugar has dissolved. Add the kumquat slices, bring to the boil and cook gently for 2-3 minutes until they are transparent.

Using a slotted spoon, remove the kumquats from the syrup and arrange them over the top of the tart. Boil the remaining syrup until the surface is covered in bubbles, then pour it over the kumquats. Leave to cool.

CITRUS TART

SERVES 6

FOR THE PASTRY
140 g/5 oz flour
85 g/3 oz butter, cut into small pieces
30 g/1 oz caster sugar
2 egg yolks

FOR THE FILLING
finely grated zest and juice of 2 unwaxed limes
finely grated zest and juice of 1 unwaxed orange
finely grated zest and juice of 1 unwaxed lemon
3 eggs + 1 extra yolk
115 g/4 oz caster sugar
150 ml/¼ pt double cream

FOR THE TOPPING
1 orange
1 lemon
1 lime
170 g/6 oz caster sugar

To make the pastry: sift the flour into a bowl, add the butter and rub it in finely with the fingertips. Stir in the sugar and egg yolks and mix together with a fork to form a firm dough.

Knead the dough on a lightly floured surface until it is smooth. Roll it out thinly and use to line a 24 cm/9½ in diameter loose-based fluted tart tin. Chill for 30 minutes.

Preheat the oven to 200C/400F/gas6.

Bake the pastry case blind for 10-15 minutes, until lightly browned at the edge and cooked at the base. Reduce the oven temperature to 160C/325F/gas3.

While the case is baking make the filling: measure 175 ml/6 fl oz of mixed fruit juice into a measuring jug, making up with water if necessary. Whisk together the eggs, egg yolk, sugar and double cream until well blended. Stir in the measured juices and the zest, mix well and pour into the pastry case.

Bake in the cooler oven for 50-55 minutes, until the filling has just set. Allow to cool in the tin before removing.

Make the topping: peel the fruits with a sharp knife, making sure that all the white pith is removed. Slice the fruits thinly.

Place the sugar in a saucepan with 150 ml/¼ pt water. Heat gently, stirring occasionally, until the sugar has dissolved. Add the lemon and lime slices to the syrup and bring them to the boil. Using a slotted spoon, remove the fruit slices from the syrup and arrange them with the orange slices over the tart.

Boil the syrup for 1-2 minutes, until the surface is full of bubbles. Pour it over the tart and allow to cool.

The term FRANGIPANE *was first used in the 18th century for pâtisserie fillings flavoured with essence of almond oil and orange flower water.*

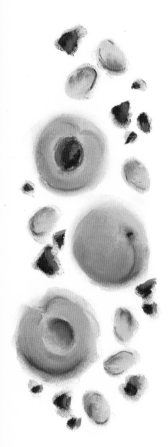

APRICOT CHOCOLATE TART

SERVES 6

FOR THE PASTRY
170 g/6 oz flour
115 g/4 oz butter, cut into small pieces
30 g/1 oz caster sugar
1 tsp almond essence
1 egg
FOR THE FILLING
2 egg yolks
85 g/3 oz caster sugar
45 g/1½ oz flour
300 ml/½ pt milk
30 g/1 oz plain chocolate
4 tbsp double cream
450 g/1 lb apricots, halved
15 g/½ oz flaked almonds, toasted
4 tbsp apricot jam

To make the pastry: sift the flour into a bowl, add the butter and rub it in finely with the fingertips. Stir in the sugar, almond essence and egg and mix together with a fork to form a firm dough.

Knead the dough on a lightly floured surface until it is smooth. Roll it out thinly and use to line a 23 cm/9 in diameter loose-based fluted tart tin. Chill for 30 minutes.

Preheat the oven to 200C/400F/gas6.

Bake the pastry case blind for 15-20 minutes, until lightly browned at the edge.

While the case is baking make the filling: in a bowl, whisk together the egg yolks, one-third of the sugar, the flour and 1 tablespoon of the measured milk until smooth. In a saucepan, bring the remaining milk and the chocolate to the boil, whisking, and pour over the egg mixture, whisking continuously. Return the mixture to the saucepan and cook gently, whisking well, until the custard has thickened.

Remove the saucepan from the heat and whisk in the cream. Pour the custard into the pastry case and leave until cold.

Place the remaining sugar in a saucepan with 5 tablespoons of water and bring to the boil, stirring. Add the apricot halves, cover and cook gently for 2-3 minutes until tender. Using a slotted spoon, remove the apricots from the syrup and arrange them over the custard filling. Scatter over the almonds.

Add the apricot jam to the syrup in the saucepan and bring to the boil. Boil for 1 minute, then sieve into a bowl. Leave to cool slightly.

Pour the apricot syrup evenly over the apricots to glaze and then leave until cold.

PRUNE AND ARMAGNAC TART

SERVES 6

FOR THE PASTRY
115 g/4 oz flour
85 g/3 oz butter, cut into small pieces
30 g/1 oz caster sugar
1 egg yolk
FOR THE FILLING
20 stoned no-soak prunes
4 tbsp Armagnac or brandy
1 tbsp clear honey
1 tbsp demerara sugar
125 ml/4 fl oz double cream
2 eggs
30 g/1 oz hazelnuts, halved
TO DECORATE
icing sugar

To make the pastry: sift the flour into a bowl, add the butter and rub it in finely with the fingertips. Stir in the sugar and egg yolk and mix together with a fork to form a firm dough.

Knead the dough on a lightly floured surface until it is smooth. Roll it out thinly and use to line a 20 cm/8 in diameter loose-based fluted tart tin. Chill for 30 minutes.

Preheat the oven to 200C/400F/gas6.

Bake the pastry case blind for 10-15 minutes, until lightly browned at the edge and cooked at the base.

While the case is baking make the filling: place the prunes and Armagnac or brandy in a small saucepan and warm through gently until hot, taking care not to over-heat. Cover and leave until cold.

Beat the honey, sugar, cream and eggs together until well blended. Strain the Armagnac or brandy into the mixture and place the prunes in the pastry case.

Stir the filling, pour it over the prunes and return the tart to the oven for 20 minutes. Scatter the hazelnuts over the tart and return it to the oven for a further 10 minutes, or until the filling has set.

Dust with icing sugar and serve warm or cold.

ROSÉ PEAR TART

SERVES 6

FOR THE PASTRY
115 g/4 oz flour
85 g/3 oz butter, cut into small pieces
55 g/2 oz walnuts, finely chopped
30 g/1 oz caster sugar
1 egg

FOR THE FILLING
300 ml/½ pt rosé wine
200 g/7 oz caster sugar
5 small pears, peeled, quartered and cored
2 egg yolks
45 g/1½ oz flour
1 tbsp rose water
300 ml/½ pt milk
4 tbsp double cream
2 tsp powdered gelatine

To make the pastry: sift the flour into a bowl, add the butter and rub it in finely with the fingertips. Stir in the walnuts, sugar and egg and mix together with a fork to form a firm dough.

Knead the dough until smooth. Roll it out thinly and use to line a 20 cm/8 in square loose-based fluted tart tin. Chill for 30 minutes.

Preheat the oven to 200C/400F/gas6.

Bake the pastry case blind for 15-20 minutes, until lightly browned at the edges.

While the case is baking make the filling: place the wine and 175 g/6 oz of the sugar in a saucepan and heat gently, stirring until the sugar has dissolved. Add the pears and bring to the boil. Cover and cook very gently for 10-15 minutes, until the pears are tender. Leave to cool.

In a bowl, whisk together the egg yolks, remaining sugar, the flour and rose water until smooth. Bring the milk to the boil in a saucepan and pour it over the egg mixture, whisking all the time. Return the mixture to the saucepan and cook gently, whisking well, until the custard has thickened. Remove from the heat and whisk in the cream. Pour into the pastry case and leave to cool.

Using a slotted spoon, transfer the pears to a large plate. Blend the gelatine with 2 tablespoons of water and stir this into the wine syrup until dissolved. Leave until almost set.

Meanwhile, cut half of the pear quarters into about 4 thin slices each, keeping the quarters together with the rounded sides on the right hand side. Slice the remaining pear quarters in the same way, with the rounded sides on the left.

Arrange 5 of the pear quarters on the custard filling and press lightly to spread them evenly; place another 5 quarters cut in the other direction and spread similarly. Repeat the process with the remaining pear halves in different directions.

When the jelly has begun to set, spoon it over the pears and chill until set. Remove from the tin.

ROSEMARY TARTE TATIN

SERVES 8

225 g/8 oz frozen puff pastry, defrosted
butter, for greasing
FOR THE FILLING
115 g/4 oz unsalted butter
170 g/6 oz caster sugar
2 tbsp clear honey
6 dessert apples, peeled, quartered and cored
finely grated zest of 1 unwaxed lemon
2 tbsp fresh rosemary

On a lightly floured surface roll the puff pastry out to a 20 cm/8 in round and place this on a large plate. Prick the surface with a fork and chill it until the filling is ready. Grease a 20 cm/8 in diameter sandwich tin with butter and line the base with greaseproof paper.

To make the filling: place the butter, sugar and honey in a non-stick frying pan and heat gently, stirring occasionally, until lightly browned and syrupy.

Add the apples, lemon zest and rosemary to the syrup and cook fairly rapidly, stirring and turning the apples in the syrup until tender.

Using a slotted spoon, transfer the apples to the prepared tin. Boil the syrup for 1-2 minutes, until thick and bubbly. Pour over the apples and leave until cold.

Preheat the oven to 200C/400F/gas6. Place the pastry round over the filling in the tin and bake for 20 minutes, or until the pastry is golden brown. Allow to cool in the tin for 15 minutes, then invert on a serving plate with a rim and remove the paper. Serve hot or warm.

Clockwise from the top: Normandy Apple Tart (page 52);
Rosemary Tarte Tatin; Rosé Pear Tart (page 49)

TARTE TATIN *is named after 'Les demoiselles Tatin', the Tatin sisters who were the local hotel-keepers at Lamotte-Beuvron in the Sologne area of the Loire. It was their speciality and was arguably the first upside-down apple tart. The sisters cooked the tart in a metal oven placed over charcoal which gave the dish its characteristic caramelled buttery apples and light crisp pastry.*

NORMANDY APPLE TART

FOR THE PASTRY
140 g/5 oz flour
85 g/3 oz butter, cut into small pieces
30 g/1 oz caster sugar
2 egg yolks
FOR THE FILLING
115 g/4 oz unsalted butter, softened
125 g/4½ oz caster sugar
3 egg yolks
2 tbsp double cream
115 g/4 oz ground almonds
2 tbsp crumbled lavender heads
4 dessert apples, peeled, halved and cored
4 tbsp apricot jam, boiled and sieved

Normandy, being the apple-growing region of France, strongly features apples in its traditional cookery. There are many variations of this traditional tart and the addition of the sweet scent of lavender is particularly rewarding.

To make the pastry: sift the flour into a bowl, add the butter and rub it in finely with the fingertips. Stir in the sugar and egg yolks and mix to a firm dough.

Knead the dough until it is smooth. Roll it out thinly and use to line a 23 cm/9 in diameter loose-based fluted tart tin. Chill for 30 minutes.

Preheat the oven to 200C/400F/gas6.

To make the filling: in a bowl, beat together the butter and 115 g/4 oz of the sugar until light and fluffy. Add the egg yolks one at a time, beating well after each. Stir in the cream and fold in the almonds.

Scatter the lavender over the base of the pastry case. Then spread the mixture over these.

Slice the apple halves very thinly, keeping the halves together. Place one half in the centre of the filling and arrange the remaining 7 evenly around it. Press each apple half gently to spread out the slices.

Bake for 15 minutes, then sprinkle the remaining sugar over the apples. Reduce the oven temperature to 180C/350F/gas4 and bake for a further 40-45 minutes, until the filling is lightly browned.

Allow to cool before removing the tart from the tin. Brush the top evenly with the apricot jam glaze.

ROSE CUSTARD TARTS

MAKES 8

FOR THE PASTRY
115 g/4 oz flour
85 g/3 oz butter or margarine, cut into small pieces
55 g/2 oz ground almonds
55 g/2 oz caster sugar
1 egg, beaten
FOR THE FILLING
2 eggs + 2 extra yolks
2 tbsp rose water
1 tbsp flour
175 ml/6 fl oz milk
300 ml/½ pt single cream
225 g/8 oz wild strawberries or stoned cherries

To make the pastry: sift the flour into a bowl. Add the butter or margarine and rub it in finely with the fingertips. Stir in the ground almonds, sugar and egg and mix with a fork to form a firm dough.

Knead the dough on a lightly floured surface until it is smooth. Roll it out thinly, and use to line eight 11 cm/4½ in loose-based fluted tart tins. Chill for 30 minutes.

Preheat the oven to 200C/400F/gas6.

Bake the pastry cases blind for 10-15 minutes, until lightly browned at the edges. Reduce the oven temperature to 180C/350F/gas4.

Place the eggs, egg yolks, rose water and flour in a bowl and whisk until smooth. Whisk in the milk and cream and pour the mixture into the pastry cases. Dot with the fruit.

Return the tarts to the cooler oven for 45-50 minutes, until the custard has just set. Allow to cool.

A Rose Custard Tart

SWEET TARTS

An amalgamation of unusual textures and exciting flavour combinations characterizes the varied recipes in this chapter, from soft cheese and custard fillings studded with exotic crystallized fruits to tarts filled with chocolate mousse, mocha coffee and creamy chestnut mixtures. Again I have made some more unusual pastries by adapting recipes for traditional dishes, such as the Rhubarb and Ginger Cream Tart and the Orange Rice Tart, flavoured like a Middle-eastern rice pudding with bay leaves and orange flower water. Many of these tarts are decorated by piping whipped cream or melted chocolate attractively over the top.

Clockwise from the top left: Mocha Walnut Flan (page 57); Chocolate Mousse Tart (page 56); Chestnut Tart (page 56); Pecan Chocolate Tart (page 57)

CHOCOLATE MOUSSE TART*

SERVES 6

FOR THE PASTRY
170 g/6 oz flour
115 g/4 oz butter or margarine, cut into small pieces
30 g/1 oz caster sugar
1 egg yolk
FOR THE FILLING
170 g/6 oz plain chocolate
15 g/½ oz white chocolate
3 eggs, separated
(* see page 2 for advice on eggs)
2 tbsp dark rum

To make the pastry: sift the flour into a bowl, add the margarine or butter and rub it in finely with the fingertips. Stir in the sugar, egg yolk and 1 table-spoon of water and mix to a firm dough.

Knead the dough until it is smooth. Roll it out thinly and use to line a 36 x 10 cm/14 x 4 in loose-based fluted tranche tin. Chill for 30 minutes.

Preheat the oven to 200C/400F/gas6.

Bake the pastry case blind for 15-20 minutes, until lightly browned at the edges.

While the case is cooling make the filling: place the plain and white chocolate in separate clean, dry bowls over hot water. Stir occasionally until the chocolate has melted. Stir the egg yolks and rum into the plain chocolate until well blended and thick.

Whisk the egg whites in a clean bowl until stiff. Gradually add the egg white to the plain chocolate mixture, folding it in well after each addition.

Pour the plain chocolate mixture into the flan case, shaking gently to level. Place the melted white chocolate in a greaseproof paper piping bag, fold down the top and snip off the point.

Pipe parallel lines of white chocolate across the chocolate filling. Draw a cocktail stick across the white chocolate lines to feather them. Leave to set.

CHESTNUT TART

SERVES 6

FOR THE PASTRY
170 g/6 oz flour
85 g/3 oz butter or margarine, cut into small pieces
1 tbsp chocolate spread
FOR THE FILLING
425 g/15 oz canned unsweetened chestnut purée
200 g/7 oz fresh soft cheese
2 tbsp Marsala
115 g/4 oz white chocolate, melted
150 ml/¼ pt single cream
55 g/2 oz plain chocolate, melted
TO DECORATE
white and dark chocolate curls

To make the pastry: sift the flour into a bowl, add the butter or margarine and rub it in finely with the fingertips. Stir in the chocolate spread and 2-3 table-spoons of cold water and mix to a firm dough.

Knead the dough until it is smooth. Roll it out thinly and use to line a 23 cm/9 in diameter loose-based fluted tart tin. Chill for 30 minutes.

Preheat the oven to 200C/400F/gas6.

Bake the pastry case blind for 15-20 minutes, until lightly browned at the edges. Allow to cool on a wire rack.

While the case is cooling make the filling: place half the chestnut purée, the cheese and Marsala in a food processor and process until smooth. Stir into the white chocolate until well blended.

Place the remaining chestnut purée and the cream in the food processor and process until smooth. Add the plain chocolate and blend well.

Spread half the plain chocolate mix over the case and spread the white chocolate mix over it evenly.

Put the remaining plain chocolate mixture in a piping bag fitted with a plain nozzle. Pipe a lattice on top and decorate with chocolate curls.

MOCHA WALNUT FLAN

SERVES 6

FOR THE PASTRY
115 g/4 oz flour
85 g/3 oz butter, cut into small pieces
55 g/2 oz walnuts, finely chopped
30 g/1 oz soft light brown sugar
1 egg
FOR THE FILLING
300 ml/½ pt milk
55 g/2 oz plain chocolate
55 g/2 oz unsalted butter
1 tsp instant coffee granules
1 tbsp cornflour
2 egg yolks
2 tbsp Tia Maria
150 ml/¼ pt single cream
150 ml/¼ pt whipping cream, whipped to soft peaks
TO DECORATE
chocolate coffee beans and chocolate curls

To make the pastry: sift the flour into a bowl, add the butter and rub it in finely. Stir in the walnuts, sugar and egg and mix to a firm dough.

Knead the dough until it is smooth. Roll it out thinly and use to line a 23 cm/9 in diameter loose-based tart tin. Chill for 30 minutes.

Preheat the oven to 200C/400F/gas6.

Bake the pastry case blind for 15-20 minutes, until lightly browned at the edges.

While the case is baking make the filling: place the milk, chocolate, butter and coffee in a pan and heat gently until the chocolate has melted. Blend the cornflour, egg yolks and liqueur together, add this to the pan and bring to the boil, stirring. Cook for 1 minute.

Off the heat, stir in the cream and pour into the pastry case. Leave until cold.

Pipe the whipped cream over the tart and decorate with chocolate coffee beans and curls.

PECAN CHOCOLATE TART

SERVES 8

FOR THE PASTRY
200 g/7 oz flour
½ tsp baking powder
140 g/5 oz butter or margarine, cut into small pieces
55 g/2 oz caster sugar
grated zest of 1 unwaxed lime
1 egg
FOR THE FILLING
140 g/5 oz caster sugar
85 g/3 oz butter or margarine
2 eggs, beaten
1 tbsp cornflour
170 g/6 oz pecan nuts, ground
85 g/3 oz plain chocolate, chopped into small pieces
2 tbsp chocolate liqueur
TO DECORATE
pecan nuts

To make the pastry: sift the flour and baking powder into a bowl, add the butter or margarine and rub it in finely with the fingertips. Stir in the sugar, lime zest and egg and mix to a firm dough.

Knead the dough until it is smooth. Roll it out thinly and use to line a 25 cm/10 in tart dish, reserving the trimmings. Chill for 30 minutes.

Preheat the oven to 190C/375F/gas5.

To make the filling: place the sugar and butter or margarine in a bowl and beat until light and fluffy. Add the eggs a little at a time, beating well after each addition. Fold in the cornflour, pecan nuts, chocolate and chocolate liqueur until evenly blended.

Pour the mixture into the pastry case and use the pastry trimmings to make a lattice across the top. Bake for 40-50 minutes, or until the filling has set.

Allow to cool in the dish and decorate with pecan nuts. Serve warm or cold, cut in wedges.

For RHUBARB AND GINGER CREAM TART *use thin young 'champagne' rhubarb available early in the season. Main-crop rhubarb, with thick deep red stems and a very tart flavour, is much coarser than the early variety.* STEM GINGER, *preserved in syrup or candied, is available as a sweetmeat and may be used in many recipes.*

CRÈME BRÛLÉE TARTS

FOR THE PASTRY
170 g/6 oz flour
115 g/4 oz butter or margarine, cut into small pieces
55 g/2 oz caster sugar
white of 1 egg
FOR THE FILLING
55 g/2 oz raspberries
55 g/2 oz wild strawberries
2 eggs + 2 extra yolks
1 tbsp caster sugar
300 ml/½ pt single cream
FOR THE TOPPING
55 g/2 oz soft light brown sugar
more wild strawberries

To make the pastry: sift the flour into a bowl, add the butter or margarine and rub it in finely with the fingertips. Stir in the sugar and egg white and mix together with a fork to form a firm dough.

Knead the dough until it is smooth. Roll it out thinly and use to line four 11 cm/4½ in loose-based fluted tart tins. Chill for 30 minutes.

Preheat the oven to 200C/400F/gas6.

Bake the pastry cases blind for 10-15 minutes, until lightly browned at the edges. Reduce the oven temperature to 160C/325F/gas3.

Arrange the fruit over the bases of the pastry cases. Place the eggs, egg yolks and sugar in a bowl and whisk until smooth. Bring the cream just to the boil in a small saucepan and pour it on the eggs, whisking all the time. Strain the custard into the cases and return them to the oven for 25-30 minutes until the custard has set. Allow to cool in the tin.·

Just before serving, make the topping: preheat a hot grill and sprinkle the brown sugar over the surface of the custard tarts. Place the tarts under the grill for 1 minute to caramelize the sugar. Allow to cool, remove the tarts from the tin and decorate with the wild strawberries.

RHUBARB AND GINGER CREAM TART

FOR THE PASTRY
170 g/6 oz flour
1½ tsp ground ginger
85 g/3 oz butter, cut into small pieces
3-4 tbsp preserved stem ginger syrup
FOR THE FILLING
115 g/4 oz caster sugar
350 g/12 oz thin rhubarb, cut into 2.5 cm/1 in lengths
2 pieces of preserved stem ginger, sliced
2 eggs, separated
4 tbsp double cream
TO DECORATE
icing sugar

Make the pastry: sift the flour and ground ginger into a bowl, add the butter and rub it in finely. Stir in the ginger syrup and mix to a firm dough.

Knead the dough until it is smooth. Roll it out thinly and use to line a 23 cm/9 in diameter loose-based fluted tart tin. Chill for 30 minutes.

Preheat the oven to 200C/400F/gas6.

Bake the pastry case blind for 10-15 minutes.

While the case is baking make the filling: place half the sugar in a pan with 1 tablespoon of water. Bring to the boil, stirring until the sugar has dissolved. Add the rhubarb and cook very gently for 2-3 minutes, shaking occasionally, until barely tender.

Drain the rhubarb, reserving the juices, and arrange it with the ginger in the case. Place the egg yolks, remaining sugar and cream in a bowl and whisk together until thick. Stir in the reserved juices.

Whisk the egg whites in a bowl until stiff. Fold them into the cream mixture. Pour into the case and bake for 30-40 minutes, until just set. Dust thickly with icing sugar and serve hot or cold.

Left: Rhubarb and Ginger Cream Tart; right: Crème Brûlée Tart

PINE KERNEL TART

SERVES 8

FOR THE PASTRY
85 g/3 oz wholemeal flour
85 g/3 oz flour
85 g/3 oz butter or margarine, cut into small pieces
30 g/1 oz soft light brown sugar
3-4 tbsp sour cream
FOR THE FILLING
115 g/4 oz butter or margarine
115 g/4 oz soft light brown sugar
115 g/4 oz ground almonds
1 tbsp rice flour
2 tbsp Madeira
2 eggs
140 g/5 oz pine kernels
1 tbsp clear honey, warmed

To make the pastry: sift the flours into a bowl, add the butter or margarine and rub it in finely with the fingertips. Stir in the sugar and sour cream and mix together with a fork to form a firm dough.

Knead the dough until it is smooth. Roll it out thinly and use to line a 20 cm/8 in square loose-based fluted tart tin. Chill for 30 minutes.

Preheat the oven to 180C/350F/gas4.

To make the filling: place the butter or margarine and sugar in a bowl and beat together for 2-3 minutes until light and fluffy. Add the ground almonds, rice flour, Madeira and eggs and mix together until evenly blended. Beat until smooth and glossy. Stir in 115 g/4 oz of the pine kernels.

Put the nut filling in the pastry case, spread it evenly and smooth the top. Sprinkle with the remaining pine kernels. Bake in the oven for 60-65 minutes, until well risen and golden brown.

Allow to cool in the tin, then turn out and remove the base. Brush the top with the warmed honey and serve warm or cold, cut into 8 pieces.

SOUR CREAM AND RAISIN TART

SERVES 6

FOR THE PASTRY
170 g/6 oz flour
85 g/3 oz butter or margarine, cut into small pieces
55 g/2 oz caster sugar
3 tbsp sour cream
FOR THE FILLING
225 g/8 oz raisins
85 g/3 oz caster sugar
1 tbsp flour
1 tsp ground mixed spice
2 tsp grated zest from an unwaxed lemon
150 ml/¼ pt sour cream
2 eggs, beaten

To make the pastry: sift the flour into a bowl, add the butter or margarine and rub it in finely with the fingertips. Stir in the sugar and sour cream and mix with a fork to form a firm dough.

Knead the dough until it is smooth. Roll it out thinly and use to line a 20 cm/8 in diameter loose-based fluted tart tin, reserving the pastry trimmings for decoration. Chill for 30 minutes.

Preheat the oven to 190C/375F/gas5.

To make the filling: place the raisins in a saucepan with 150 ml/¼ pt water. Bring to the boil, cover and simmer for 3-4 minutes until tender. Stir in the sugar, flour, mixed spice and lemon zest and cook for 1 minute, stirring. Allow to cool.

In a bowl beat together the sour cream and eggs. Add the raisin mixture and stir until well blended. Pour the mixture into the pastry case. Roll the pastry trimmings out and cut them into thin strips. Decorate the tart with a lattice of pastry strips.

Bake in the oven for 45-50 minutes, until the filling has risen and is golden brown. Leave to cool in the tin, then remove carefully and serve in wedges.

ORANGE RICE TART

SERVES 12

FOR THE PASTRY
200 g/7 oz flour
115 g/4 oz butter or margarine, cut into small pieces
55 g/2 oz caster sugar
2 tsp grated zest from an unwaxed orange
1 egg, beaten
FOR THE FILLING
55 g/2 oz arborio or pudding rice
350 ml/12 fl oz milk
2 tbsp orange flower water
1 fresh bay leaf
115 g/4 oz butter
85 g/3 oz caster sugar
2 eggs, separated
4 tbsp apricot jam
2 oranges, peeled and cut into segments
TO DECORATE
1 unwaxed orange, thinly sliced

To make the pastry: sift the flour into a bowl, add the butter or margarine and rub it in finely with the fingertips. Stir in the sugar, orange zest and egg and mix together with a fork to form a firm dough.

Knead the dough on a lightly floured surface until it is smooth. Roll it out thinly and use to line a 28 x 20 cm/11 x 8 in oblong loose-based fluted tart tin. Chill for 1 hour.

To make the filling: place the rice, milk, orange flower water and bay leaf in a saucepan. Bring to the boil, stirring occasionally. Then cover and cook very slowly for 30-35 minutes, until the rice has absorbed the milk and is soft and sticky. Stand the pan in cold water to cool it quickly. Discard the bay leaf.

Preheat the oven to 180C/350F/gas4.

Beat the butter, half the sugar and the egg yolks together in a bowl. Add the rice and blend well.

Whisk the egg whites in a bowl until stiff. Add the remaining sugar a little at a time, whisking well after each addition, until stiff again. Fold this gently into the rice mixture until evenly blended.

Spread the apricot jam over the base of the pastry case and cover this with the orange segments. Top with the rice meringue filling, spreading to cover smoothly. Bake in the oven for 75-85 minutes, or until the pastry is pale golden and the filling has set.

Allow to cool in the tin and serve warm or cold decorated with the orange slices.

Pine Kernel Tart

Ricotta is an Italian whey cheese and is now readily available in this country in its fresh unripened form, when it is white and creamy with a soft slightly granular texture. It has a bland sweetish flavour and may be eaten fresh with fruit or used for cheesecakes, pastries and in savoury dishes, especially with pasta.

ITALIAN CHEESE TART

SERVES 6

FOR THE PASTRY
115 g/4 oz flour
85 g/3 oz butter or margarine, cut into small pieces
30 g/1 oz caster sugar
grated zest of 1 unwaxed lemon
white of 1 egg
FOR THE FILLING
55 g/2 oz glacé fruits, chopped
30 g/1 oz plain chocolate, chopped into small pieces
30 g/1 oz raisins
1 tbsp Marsala
225 g/8 oz Ricotta or cream cheese
30 g/1 oz caster sugar
1 egg, separated, + 1 extra yolk

To make the pastry: sift the flour into a bowl, add the butter or margarine and rub it in finely with the fingertips. Stir in the sugar, lemon zest and egg white and mix with a fork to form a firm dough.

Knead the dough until it is smooth. Roll it out thinly and use to line an 18 cm/7 in diameter loose-based fluted tart tin. Chill for 30 minutes.

Preheat the oven to 200C/400F/gas6.

Bake the pastry case blind for 10-15 minutes until lightly browned at the edges. Reduce the oven temperature to 180C/350F/gas4.

While the case is baking make the filling: place the glacé fruits, chocolate, raisins and Marsala in a bowl and stir well to mix.

Place the cheese in another bowl. Add the sugar and egg yolks and beat well. Whisk the egg white in a third bowl until stiff. Fold this into the cheese mixture, together with the mixed fruits and spread the filling over the pastry.

Bake in the cooler oven for 45-50 minutes, until the filling has set and the pastry is golden brown. Leave in the tin to cool.

BELGIAN TART

SERVES 6

FOR THE PASTRY
115 g/4 oz cream cheese
55 g/2 oz butter, softened
200 g/7 oz flour
30 g/1 oz cornflour
30 g/1 oz caster sugar
FOR THE FILLING
2 tbsp coconut strands
2 tbsp soft light brown sugar
3 tbsp apricot jam
2 nectarines, sliced
TO DECORATE
strips of fresh coconut
more nectarine slices

To make the pastry: place the cream cheese and butter in a bowl, beat until smooth. Stir in 2 tablespoons of water, the flour, cornflour and sugar and mix with a fork to form a firm dough.

Knead the dough on a lightly floured surface until it is smooth. Roll it out thinly and use two-thirds of the pastry to line a 20 cm/8 in loose-based fluted tart tin. Chill for 30 minutes.

Preheat the oven to 200C/400F/gas6.

Make the filling: shred the remaining pastry and trimmings on a coarse grater. Mix together the coconut and sugar in a bowl.

Spread the apricot jam over the base of the pastry case and cover with the sliced nectarines. Top with the grated pastry and sprinkle with the coconut mixture.

Bake in the oven for 35-40 minutes, until lightly browned. Serve warm or cold. Decorate with strips of coconut and slices of nectarine.

Left: Belgian Tart; right: Orange Rice Tart (page 61)

INDEX

Page numbers in *italic* refer to the photographs

ACKNOWLEDGEMENTS
The author would like to thank
Mavis Giles for typing her copy at all
hours, Michelle for her wonderful
work on the photography and Sue
Storey and Mary Evans for their
support.

The Publishers would like to thank
the following for the use of
accessories in the photography:

Sander Architectural Mirrors,
Sander House,
Elmore Street,
London N1.